TEENAGE KICKS

101 things to do before youre 16

CLIVE GIFFORD

Hodder
Children's
Books

A division of Hachette Children's Books

About the Author

Clive Gifford (current TK rating 1061, oh yes) is not quite all there. Anyone who has leapt out of a plane, let an elephant walk over him and spent a whole evening in a pantomime camel suit (the front half, thankfully) must be one ring tone short of a 3G mobile.

Clive has piloted a glider, raced quad bikes (he came last), visited Australia, met Test cricket legends, pulled a MacTwist on a skateboard, swum with hippos, superglued pound coins to the pavement, scored a penalty at an English Championship football club, been lawnmower racing and faked a crop circle – and that was all just last year! Further back, he has travelled to over 70 countries from Egypt to Easter Island*.

Clive is the author of over 80 books on serious and far-from-serious topics for children, teens and adults. These include *Pants Attack!*, the *So You Think You Know?* series of quiz books, *Voices: Gangs* and *World Issues: Racism.* Clive lives in Manchester, England.

www.clivegifford.co.uk

*OK, so Easter Island isn't a country, it's part of Chile, but the point is he's been around a bit, all right?

Contents

Contents

Introduction

Welcome to Teenage Kicks. Here you will find over 100 challenges for you to take on and live life to the full. They range in cost, complexity and effort. Some require nerves of steel or an iron will. Others need you to be flexible or bend over backwards to help others. At stake are 'Teenage Kicks' or 'TK' points which go to make up your final TK ranking.

To give you the general idea, turn the page to run through a challenge that didn't quite make the book . . .

Monkey Business

Teach baboons to write a bestseller.

TK-ed Off ☐ **+17** 'My monkeys have just finished writing Hairy Primate and the Banana of Doom!'

Orang-utan-ing out with humans when you could be earning far more than peanuts? Get yourself a troop of baboons, arm them with laptops and see if you can coax them into going bananas and writing a bestselling novel.

You will need a large enclosure for them, a regular order with your local greengrocer for fruit and veg and a mop and bucket for regular mucking out (urrghh). Publishing's a jungle so make sure that your baboons don't monkey around but work hard. Don't expect too much. In 2003, six crested Sulawesi macaque monkeys at Paignton Zoo in Devon were each given a typewriter and four weeks to produce a work of Shakespeare. Unfortunately, the six monkeys produced only five pages of text, mostly containing the letter S, before attacking the typewriters and doing their 'business' on them!

Little Angel (TK+8)
Donate any proceeds from sales of your bestseller to charity.

U Devil (TK+4)
Writing not going well? Write some pages yourself, pop them back in your baboon's typewriters and call the press! Alternatively, cram a small mate into a baboon suit and get him or her typing.

Blag Box
The cost of housing and feeding a troop of baboons can be prohibitive. A cheaper alternative would be to lock Clive, the author of this book, in a cage for six months. He only needs tea and toast and, a big bonus, is just about house-trained.

Challenge ratings

All four ratings are marked out of five.

 ## Cost

Gives an approximate idea of how much you'll have to fork out to take on this challenge.

 ## Courage/Fear

How much bottle you may need to carry out the challenge.

 ## Effort

An approximate measure of how much the challenge will stop you from sitting on the sofa watching *When Quantity Surveyors Turn Bad* or *Live Celebrity Nose-Picking* on the telly.

 ## Feelgood Factor

The amount of afterglow, bragging rights and general sense of fulfilment you are likely to get from completing the challenge.

TK-ed Off

The number of TK points you get for completing a challenge. Keep a note of your TK points. Once you've added them up, discover your TK ranking by finding out where your score falls on the TK ranking chart over on the next page.

 ## Little Angel

A more thoughtful and considerate challenge option to earn extra TK points. Bless.

 ## U Devil

Naughty and cheeky variations on the main theme.

 ## Blag Box

Not everyone has access to a large bank balance. This offers a cheaper and/or easier alternative to the main challenge.

TK Ranking Chart

0–71	Total Loser
72–129	Is that all you've got?
130–185	Let's call you 'feather', you're that light weight.
186–234	Come on, you can do much better than this.
235–287	Not bad, but surely, there's more you can do?
288–322	Good work
323–389	Very Good work
390–456	Great work
457–532	You're fast becoming a legend ...
533–648	Legend!
649–809	Approaching awesome ...
810–925	Fact: You ARE Awesome!
925–1200	You're scaring us now, you're THAT amazing!
1200+	You've Done It! You've Gained Maximum Teenage Kicks!

1. Let Me Entertain You

01 02 03 04

'Paging Dan Gleebitz . . . Have you seen Dan Gleebitz?'

TK-ed Off ☐ **+7** *They actually said my name over the tannoy.*

> Prank phone calls are a complete no-no. But once, just once, you should have a little fun with a fake public announcement at a shopping mall or train station.

Stake out your target area beforehand and figure out how you can get the name to the announcer without arousing suspicion. Writing it down or looking innocent and stressing different parts of the name than the funny ones as you say it will help.

Figure out the amusing name you want the world to hear. Don't be obvious and highly abusive – any announcer worth their salt will spot a four letter word in a moment. Go for unusual but feasible spellings and make sure the first name and the surname appear innocuous by themselves but are dynamite when put together. Olive Yew* and Sue Ridge* are gentle examples whilst Mike Rotchurtz* is a little racier, but I'm sure you can do better.

---

* I love you; Sewage; My crotch hurts

Spin Doctor

TK~ed Off ☐ **+9** 'I can regularly spin the ball for more than 15 seconds.'

Nothing, repeat nothing, smells of basketball or netball success quite like being able to spin the ball on your finger for fifteen seconds or longer. It doesn't matter if you've been fouled out, missed 100 shots, or run ragged by the opposition, if you can get spinning, you'll get some serious spectator respect.

1. With your arm stretched out and elbow slightly flexed, balance the ball on the pads of the five fingers of your hand.

2. Twist your wrist with a snap to the left to put spin on the ball. Bend your elbow and let the ball hop up from your fingertips just a couple of centimetres. Practise this stage and remember, the bigger the snap of your wrist, the more spin you generate which makes the ball easier to balance.

3. Aim for the ball to land on your index finger at the bottom and centre of the ball so that it can balance.

4. You have two options for keeping the spin going. You can either drop the ball back on to your fingertips to repeat Stage 2 onwards, or ideally, you slap the ball carefully with your left hand two or three times to keep it spinning.

Rock Your World

Find a way to get on stage with a band, no matter what your musical ability.

TK-ed Off ☐ +13

Less pop idol and more bone idle? Have about as much musical talent as a tone-deaf cabbage? Fear not, the great music revolution means that there are plenty of ways you can still get on stage! Try our top five countdown.

5. Pick a band that are playing live soon, ideally one which contains good friends of yours. Start hanging out with them, bigging up their musical compositions.

4. Make yourself indispensable. It might just be fetching and carrying for them, making gig fliers or lending them something they want – from your Mum's old keyboard to your Dad and his white van. In return, explain your desire to go on stage with them.

3. Work on your role on stage. Most fledgling bands can't afford clever electronic wizardry but often have one great musician who comes up with the songs. He or she may get frustrated that they lack enough sets of hands to play scorching lead guitar, set off a mock police siren and bang two saucepan lids together all at the same time. Be their extra hands. Offer to do something that contributes to the sound of a few songs.

2. If the band have the word 'collective', 'posse', 'gang' or 'massive' in their title, argue that they need to look the part and need extra bods on stage to add to the vibe. Argue your case: Bez never played a note of music in his life, but he was a star with the Happy Mondays (ask your Dad) for his manic dancing.

1. On the night, look the part, dress like the band and exude confidence throughout. Look like you're a vital cog in the band's machine even when you've nothing to do. And when it's finally time for you to leave the stage, milk the moment and leave with a flourish having rocked your world.

Little Angel (TK+14)

If you're a budding musician into just about any flava of music, then you really, really should play live properly and do it at a young age, it is such a buzz.

GoooaaaalllLLL!

🛍 ⓞⓞⓞⓞⓞ 😗 ●ⓞⓞⓞⓞ 😆 ●●●ⓞⓞ 👍 ●●●ⓞⓞ

TK~ed Off ☐ **+8** for any memorable goal celebration.

Whether you're playing hockey, rugby or football, treat yourself to a slice of serious showboating with a tailor-made goal celebration. Yes, you might get an earwigging from your coach, but if you keep your shirt on and keep your move quick and not rude or provocative, you should get away with it. Some old and new school moves are below but why not see if you can make up your own?

Old School Moves
The Shearer – Wheel away with one arm and hand raised to the crowd – no rude gestures, now. (TK -1, you really should be able to do better than that).

The Aquaplane – Got a nice wet and soft pitch? Go on a run and in plenty of space dive forward and glide along the skiddy, muddy ground with your upper chest and head raised and your arms out. Highly recommended, especially if it's someone else's turn to do the washing. (TK+5 plus 1 point per metre travelled on the ground.)

New School Moves

The Robo-Crouch – Dance like a robot from 1984 ... not on your nelly. Peter Crouch's 2006 move is so old hat it's not true. Best avoided.

Flipping Marvellous – For serious gymnasts only, backflips, somersaults and spins can top off a memorable goal. Nigerian striker Julius Aghahowa favours the six flips and a double somersault all in a row. A forward roll which ends with you back on your feet saluting the imaginary 50,000 crowd is perfectly acceptable.

> **Warning: Make sure the ref has given the goal before you celebrate!**

An Audience With ... You!

●○○○○   ●○○○○   ●●○○○   ●●○○○

TK~ed Off ☐ **+6** for getting in a TV audience.

TK~ed Off ☐ **+2** for your family recording your face on telly.

TK~ed Off ☐ **+9** for getting a speaking part on telly.

> Fancy yourself as a budding TV star? Well we can't guarantee you'll be hosting your own show next year but with a bit of luck you should get on TV as an audience member or more!

Happy Clappers

Many TV production companies are crying out for well-behaved live audience members who smile, laugh and clap on demand. You'll need patience as a 30-minute show may take two or three hours to record, but it can be fascinating to see a show's stars off guard and how a TV programme is put together. Plus you get to see a new episode months before your mates. Try to get a seat near an aisle if the show is interactive, as presenters who do go into the audience often can't be bothered to go further than the first couple of seats either side of the aisle. It goes without saying that you should record the show so you can sift through afterwards for any shots of you in the audience.

Vox Pop

An alternative is to keep abreast of your local news via newspapers and local sites and look out for upcoming events likely to prompt local TV news teams to head into your neighbourhood, especially stories affecting schools and children. Do your homework on the news story, get there early and see if you can be singled out for a 'person on the street' interview, known in TV land as a 'vox pop'.

Telly Web

There are lots of places on the internet to head to learn more – some of the best are below.

http://www.radioandtelly.co.uk/tvaudience.html
A great opening guide with a collection of contact details for TV shows.

http://www.tvrecordings.com/
Excellent free audience ticket site for shows recorded in London.

http://www.itv.com/BeonTV/Tickets/default.html
Tickets for many ITV shows in Manchester, Yorkshire and elsewhere can be sorted from this site.

Brush your teeth beforehand. No one wants to see spinach-covered choppers on telly!

Ham It Up

🪙 ⭘⭘⭘⭘⭘ 😠 ●●●⭘⭘ 😬 ●●⭘⭘⭘ 👍 ●●⭘⭘⭘

TK~ed Off ☐ +15

> **Liven up your snooze-some school play with a prank or some serious upstaging.**

Unless you've got a big part, appearing in a school play is like a long day trip to the British seaside. It starts out as a good idea but the journey there is so tedious that you've lost interest by the time you've arrived. The majority of parts in school plays are walk-on roles or ones which require you to speak one or two lines. Yet, you have to turn up day-in, day-out as others hog the limelight. Honestly, it's enough to make you spit.

So what can you do? Well, with an active imagination and a sense of mischief, it's more a case of what you can't. Don't jeopardize the whole play or risk injury.
The fun and skill is to do or set up something that lasts a brief moment and is funny and is then gone.
Let's take you through a couple of examples.

Noises Off!

If you're forced into a nativity, record or download some samples of sheep and possibly, more exotic animals, on to a digital music player. Under your robes as a wise man, shepherd or peasant, no one will spot your player attached to battery-powered speakers. Choose your moment to set volume to maximum and blast out the baaaaaaa!

The End

Many plays feature bit-part actors dying or sleeping in scenes. If you're one of those unfortunates who have to lie there for ages, ham up your role. If you're sleeping, break into a loud snore. If you die on stage, take a bit longer than you should to finally expire. Throw in lots of groaning, side-clutching and eye-rolling to get maximum laughs before you finally cop it.

U Devil ~ Pin Up

It's a cheap shot but with lots of luvvie hugging before a play, it's painfully easy to stick a piece of paper with, 'Poor Actor', 'I Smell' or whatever most suits to the back of someone else's costume without them suspecting.

Blag Box

A stack of free sound effect downloads can be found here:
www.partnersinrhyme.com/pir/PIRsfx.shtml

Carry ʌOK
ᵃ ᵗᵘⁿᵉ

Karaoke tips for the hopeless.

TK-ed Off ☐ +19 I sang even though I'm not a good singer.

> If you're a school choir star and love nothing more
> than to belt out a tune, turn the page. But if you
> truly cannot carry a tune, you should give it a go at
> a live karaoke session on holiday or somewhere
> else where your school friends aren't present.

♪ 'Do'

Pick a suitable song. You're no R'n'B diva so focus on a song which doesn't require soaring vocals. An up-tempo number with as few long notes as possible is far easier to carry off than a slow, smoochy ballad. Avoid rap as if you get half a beat or word behind, you'll be left lost in a massive jumble of words.

♪ 'Re'

Learn the words in advance. Knowing the lyrics inside-out will remove one cause of concern for you, leaving you able to concentrate on the rest of your performance.

♪ 'Mi'

Explain your worries to a friendly KJ (karaoke jockey) in advance and he may give you a go on his machine in private or be able to adjust the echo and reverb on his amp to help improve the sound of your vocals.

♪ 'Fa'

Never touch the microphone with your mouth or face. Keep it 3-5cm from your mouth. And, no, don't start lassoing audience members by swinging the microphone lead around your head.

♪ 'So'

If your song contains some long notes, start with the microphone further away from you and slowly bring the microphone closer as you hold the note. This has the effect of making the note sound stronger and more consistent as your voice starts to weaken as you hold a long note.

♪ 'La'

If you simply cannot reach a note, don't go and murder it, pull the mic away from you and mouth the word or turn your head seemingly overcome with emotion or your performance.

♪ 'Ti'

Don't just sing, perform. No one's expecting the perfect voice, so give them something to enjoy other than your dubious singing. Dance a bit, smile, enjoy it. After all, you've got up there and are giving it a go.

♪ 'Do'

If you enjoy the experience, why not try singing lessons? Many singing coaches specialise in working with beginners.

Read A Bunch Of Boss Books

●●○○○ ●○○○○ ●●●○○ ●●●○○

TK~ed Off ☐ **+5** for every book you read cover to cover.

Well, you're halfway through one, aren't you? (Yeah, right.)

Other books, mags and websites lecture you about reading their top 10, 20 or 100 literary masterpieces (in their opinion). I thought about it. I even started to draw up a list but after getting to No.14 *Skellig* by David Almond, I thought, this is nonsense, you're an individual, who am I to say what you should read?

To tell you the truth, the publishers went nuts. They threatened me with a big stick and stopped my milk and biscuits allowance, but I refuse to waver (or should that be wafer). Look, there are hundreds of great books out there. Just read some, eh?

Don't let a book's image put you off. You may be surprised. Many books by famous, glamorous and exciting celebs are deadly dull. Lots of books by crusty old authors born centuries ago are racy and exciting. A book that adults say is 'vital' can give you the creeps. A book they dismiss as 'pointless' or 'rubbish' can be the best thing you've read.

Whatever read you plump for, stick with it. Some books start slow or confusing but get better. Not all mind, but many. Don't be embarrassed to ask someone to explain anything that confuses you. I do that all the time and I am so old, I was once lying down on a beach and a kid cried, 'Look, Dad, a fossil'.

If you're stumped for what to read, ask around, particularly your friends, a kindly librarian or a teacher you can actually stand. If you do like lists, check out the lists below.

Cover Yourself

Tough guy who doesn't want to be seen reading Jane Austen? Deep, serious type not wanting to be caught with the latest Captain Underpants? You're not alone. Harry Potter books come in serious cover versions for adults fearful of being caught reading a kids' book. Ridiculous really but if it bothers you, simply cover the book in paper or buy a stretchable book cover from a place such as www.bookaroocovers.com.

Top Books Lists

http://www.bbc.co.uk/arts/bigread/top100.shtml
http://www.time.com/time/2005/100books/
http://books.guardian.co.uk/top10s/top10/0,,1942424,00.html

Unmask a Miser

🪙 ●○○○○   😈 ○○○○○   🙂 ●●○○○   👍 ●●●○○

TK-ed Off ☐ **+7** for a miser on camera trying to lever a coin off of the pavement.

TK-ed Off ☐ **+14** for every additional time you catch them out in the same way.

Really short arms but long pockets? First in the queue for ice cream, last in the queue to pay? We all know a cheapskate or miser. It is your teenage duty to teach such tight-wallets a lesson. Here's how.

1. You need to pick a quiet place where your target miser will walk along. Invite them over and offer free food or toys. Misers love free stuff.

2. Use strong glue to glue a coin, not your fingers, on to the pavement. Choose the lowest value coin you reckon they'll still scrabble for. A Euro? 50p? How low will they go? 'Cos the lower the dough, the more it's a no, no!

3. Stake out your target area with a clear camera view and hide behind a tree or below an upstairs window.

4. Make sure your digicam is running and stifle any laughs as the miser tries to prize the coin off the pavement. Many digital cameras have a video mode as well as being able to take photos. Video is great but a sequence of snaps run out on your inkjet printer. Show them the video or slip a few snaps into their schoolbag – what you do next is up to you.

U Devil (TK+3)

Got a tech-head friend? Get them to run up the best picture as a screensaver for a PC or go for the full-on multimedia presentation!

What's a miser's favourite clothing gift?
Anything you give them which contains big checks!

Five A Day

TK~ed Off ☐ +6 'I played five a day.'

TK~ed Off ☐ +4 for any event you win.

> By the time the 2012 Olympics are here, you'll probably be over 16 and trying to be a desperately sensible and stuffy adult. Shame. Until then, you still have the chance to roll back the years and play an old-school playground pentathlon. There are seven games below, pick five to play from.

Conker~ing
Sneak out of sight (the back of the bike sheds was the 1950s favourite) for some hard conkering action. Strings on your conkers should be 25cm or so long and you mustn't move as your opponent goes to strike.

Hopscotch
The excellent www.gameskidsplay.net/ website describes hopscotch in detail as well as listing dozens of other 'old school' games.

Any old Rope
Skipping isn't just for girls, it's an endurance sport – try skipping for 200 turns of the rope and you'll see what we mean, plus you can have skipping races over 100m of grass.

Losing Your Marbles
There are lots of different games, like Conqueror (hitting another person's marble means winning it off them) and Ring Taw

(knocking marbles out of a ring). Check out the BBC's handy webpage on the subject at www.bbc.co.uk/dna/h2g2/A683660

Wall-ey

Take one football, one section of wall and any number of players and take turns to hit the wall with the ball. If you miss with your kick, you're out. Look to hit at an angle to send the ball away at an impossible angle for your opponent to strike.

Stuck in the Mud

An advanced game of tag or 'It' which needs lots of people and a marked out space i.e. a netball court. Once you've been tagged you stand still with your legs apart. You can only be unfrozen by someone crawling through your legs.

H N V

Not the music store chain, but the legendary footballing pastime, Headers and Volleys, responsible for more dented cars in the 1950s and 60s Britain than any other. Play in plenty of space with the keeper scoring two points for every goal attempt missed or saved and the outfield players scoring five points for every header or genuine volley scored.

Little Angel (TK+6)

Go the whole hog and make it a class project to spend the day as you might in the 1950s. Others though, might not thank you for the fish paste sandwiches they get at lunchtime.

U Devil

Choose your conker with care beforehand. One that floats in water is likely to be soft and damaged inside. Battle harden it the night before by soaking it in vinegar and baking it for a short while in the oven.

Feeling Fruity

TK-ed Off □ +6

**Show the apple of your eye his or her very own personalized apple.
Beats flowers or chocs any day.**

Just like successful relationships, you need long term commitment for this one, oh and access to a red apple tree. Consult the owner as to when the apples are almost fully grown but yet to ripen. Cut out the initials of your loved or lusted one from sticky backed plastic or a piece of polythene and stick on to an unripe green apple. Now sit back and wait a few weeks or months until the apple ripens, peel off the letters and bingo, you can feel fruity.

U Devil

Passion dies, crushes change. Hedge your bets and cover a dozen apples with different letters of the alphabet just in case. If you haven't got that much access to apples, go with a love heart shape on a couple of apples which can work for anyone.

Learn to Juggle

TK~ed Off ☐ **+25** for managing to juggle a three ball cascade.

> As the clumsiest, most cack-handed person in the world, trust me when I say learning to juggle is easy if you are determined. You need to de-program how you normally throw and catch a ball. Regular practice can see you juggling the classic three ball cascade in a couple of weeks.

1. Start with balls. Your hands will start a little wider than your body and move inwards to scoop-throw the ball up and across gently. The ball should peak just above head height and fall so that your catching hand has to move as little as possible.

2. Now the crucial part. Don't throw both balls at the same time. Throw the second ball just as the first peaks in the air. As your second ball reaches its peak, the first ball should have landed in your left hand.

3. This will feel weird but keep at it day-in and day-out. At first just practise swapping the two balls (i.e. two throws and two catches). Then, keep them moving by scoop-throwing any ball that lands in your hand back up and across trying to keep your throws and catches in rhythm. Counting can help.

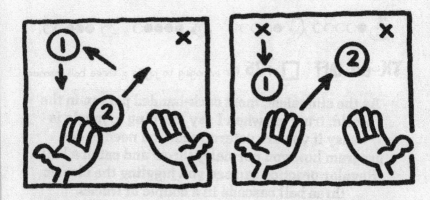

4. Now for the third ball. Put two balls in the hand you tend to start your two ball cascade with. The ball nearest your fingertips is thrown first, then the ball in your other hand and finally, the second ball in your first hand. Try to throw all three balls just like that without worrying about catching them. Count one-two-three to time their release.

5. Gradually, work at catching the balls and throwing them back up and across. Don't worry if it doesn't come at first and don't tense up and try to throw them harder or faster. Try to keep your hands down

and relaxed as this gives you a little bit of extra time to throw and catch the balls.

U Devil: Simple Tricks

Tired from all of this hard work? Keep on juggling, keep your back straight and start to bend your knees so that you can have a nice sit down *and* juggle.

Try to bounce one ball off your forearm or knee or your held-taut t-shirt to rebound it back into the air to keep juggling – always draws an appreciative 'oooh' from an audience.

Blag Box

Don't buy expensive juggling balls. Seek out a set at a charity or pound shop or use the toe ends of three old socks filled with split peas or lentils and sewn up securely with stout thread. Make sure the socks are washed beforehand. Cheesy!

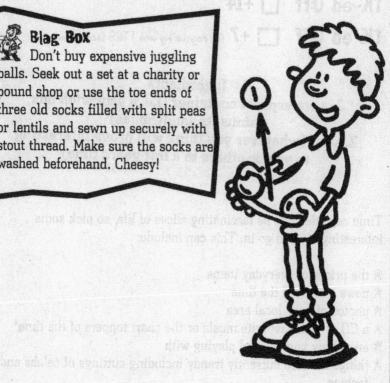

Buried Pleasure

Bury a time capsule and more.

TK~ed Off ☐ +14

TK~ed Off ☐ +7 for registering with ITCS (see below).

> ## Ingredients
> 1. a waterproof container (i.e. a sandwich box minus its sandwiches)
> 2. stuff (whatever you think will prove interesting to you or others in a few years time)

Time capsules can be fascinating slices of life, so pick some interesting stuff to go in. This can include:

※ the prices of everyday items
※ news stories of the time
※ photos of your local area
※ a CD of your favourite music or the chart toppers of the time*
※ an old toy you enjoyed playing with
※ things that are currently trendy including cuttings of celebs and fashion
※ details in permanent marker pen about you and your family.

*Although in 20 or 30 year's time, who's to say anyone will have a CD player!

Seal everything in a plastic freezer bag and use strong parcel tape to additionally seal the outside of the container. Use permanent marker to write your name, the burial date and date you'd like it opened. GET PERMISSION to bury it in a deep enough hole not to be disturbed every time Auntie Joan does some weeding.

Now make a map and take photos of its exact position and store carefully. If you're not too bothered about the time capsule being opened on a set date, you could have some fun by making a cryptic treasure map with clues explaining where and what it is and just leave it behind a dusty old book on explorers or similar in your local library. You never know, a kid in the future might get a huge thrill seeking out your capsule.

Register your capsule with the International Time Capsule Society. No, it's not a hoax, more a serious attempt to keep track of buried treasure over the ages. Their webpages are a bit stuffy but do include some fabulous stories: http://www.oglethorpe.edu/about_us/crypt_of_civilization/international _time_capsule_society.asp

What do you call a man burying a time capsule in a deep hole using a spade? Doug!

Out of the Box

TK-ed Off ☐ +5

We'll keep this one short. Think of all the time you spend sitting in front of the goggle box watching people doing something really enjoyable. It might be a sport like motocross or tennis, a music talent show, dancing, acting or a nature programme. Ever wished you could be doing what they're doing? Stop watching it, chatting about it and start to do it. There's no point letting your childhood pass by with you still wondering 'what if . . .' Of course, you have to start small and work your way up, but that's all part of the fun. Join a sports team or take a dance class, find a place that does comedy and acting or music lessons. However good or bad you turn out to be isn't the point. Just enjoy it.

Flick of the Wrist

Wow others on the beach by throwing a flying disc long, straight and far.

TK~ed Off

☐ **+7** for a good backhand

☐ **+7** for a sidearm

☐ **+7** for a hammer

We've all limply tossed a flying disc, watching it wobble away and miss the target by miles. In my case there's no excuse, especially as I played in the European Frisbee Club Championships in Gothenberg, Sweden. But then, a lot of people were off sick and I think the selectors got the wrong number ...

Backhander

Most people throw a frisbee from their stomach. Wrong. Think like a backhand shot in tennis. Stand feet apart with the shoulder of your throwing arm facing the front. Grip the edge of the disc so that your forefinger lies along the outside rim, the other fingers are inside the disc and your thumb lies along the top. Cock your wrist back as you swing back.

Swing forwards from your elbow with the left edge of the disc pointing slightly down (this helps it fly flat and straight, don't ask me why, it's physics). Snap your wrist sharply to release the disc with lots of spin – most of the throw's power comes from the wrist. This won't go well at first, but after a couple of practice sessions, you should get the disc spinning away flat and true making it reach its target.

The Sidearm

The daddy of throws and proof you know your stuff, the sidearm or forearm throw takes a while to master but looks awesome. Grip the disc and stand as shown in the picture. Try to keep your grip slightly loose. Cock your wrist back and extend your arm out from your body. Let the outer edge of the disc tilt towards the ground a little. Uncock your wrist with a snap and the disc should spin off your middle finger. Experiment with the amount of tilt needed to send the disc flying away level to the ground.

Hammer Time

The hammer is an overhead throw which sends the disc slicing through the air. Eventually, the disc bottoms out and drops like a stone to the ground. Using the sidearm grip, raise the disc over your head, slightly tilted to the left. Bring your arm back slightly and then throw it forward and slightly upwards. Snap your wrist and release the disc over and slightly in front of your head. Watch it cut through the air before bottoming out.

Catch Up

Catch the disc two-handed until you gain confidence in reading how it rises and falls on the air. Then, try a few trick catches from behind the back or jumping up and catching it between your legs. If you're a boy, careful with this one for obvious reasons!

The Ultimate Sport

Ultimate is a fast, action-packed seven- or five-a-side team sport played with a flying disc by dozens of teams in the UK and hundreds more elsewhere. Visit UK Ultimate's website (www.ukultimate.com) or head to http://www.whatisultimate.com/ for more information.

Child's Play: Enjoy Your Toys

Childhood is desperately short. You're bombarded with advertising and images urging you to grow up and to dress, speak and act like an adult. That's fine, but let me assure you it's not all sunny once you get there. Adulthood comes with responsibilities, bills, work (like school but longer hours) and bills. Have I mentioned bills? Good. Many adults spend a sizeable chunk of their lives wishing they were still a child. Lecture over. Embrace being a kid, enjoy your toys and go on playing games.

TK-ed Off

Score two points for each of the following you do after reading this book.

☐ Have a HUGE game of hide and seek involving as many people as possible.

☐ Enjoy toys you're growing out of one more time before getting rid of them.

☐ Make a snowman and have an epic snowball fight.

☐ Spend a whole rainy day during school holidays playing a marathon board game or race car session.

☐ Spend an age with friends dressing up in fancy dress.

☐ Have a memorable water pistol shootout during the summer.

☐ Dive into the mud and get filthy – but only if you promise to wash your clothes afterwards.

☐ Get as much action on bouncy castles as possible (adult ones are really rare).

Classic Toy Trivia

There are more than 400,000 million LEGO bricks and parts in existence. 400,000 million and 1 if you find that one down the back of the sofa.

Barbie's full name is actually Barbara Millicent Roberts.

The first World Championship for Scalextric racing took place in London in 1964.

It's a Small World

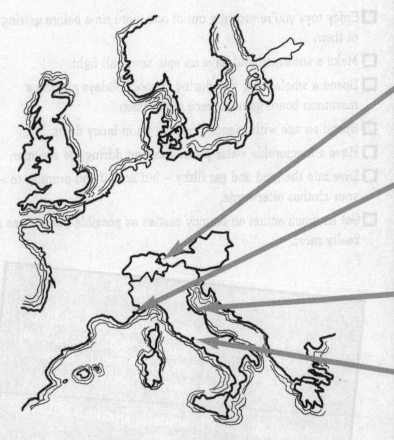

Enjoy yourself in one or more of the world's smallest nations whilst on your holidays.

TK-ed Off ☐ **+11** per microstate visited.

Europe has four of the world's six microstates (smallest nations) – Liechtenstein, Monaco, San Marino and Vatican City. All are located close to or within popular holiday hotspots like Italy and France. Look to visit one of these dolls-house sized countries on holiday.

Liechtenstein (area: 160km^2)

Have a wander around the country's charming capital city, Vaduz and check out its skiing museum, its fabulous art museum or, next to the tourist office, its rather less fabulous single-room postage stamp museum.

Monaco (area: 2km^2)

A tax haven for the fabulously wealthy, you can visit its lavish aquarium and the cathedral which holds the graves of its princes and princesses. You can also get a cool, overpriced drink, put on your trendy shades and hang out beachside with the millionaires, starlets and beautiful people of Europe.

San Marino (area: 61km^2)

Visit the castle fortress, check out a medieval crossbow tournament or climb to the top of this tiny republic's one mountain, Mount Titano. From there, you can see almost the entire country.

Vatican City (area: 0.44 km^2)

The home of the Pope is situated within Rome. Check out any members of the Swiss Guard, Vatican's just over 100-strong army. Also hop from one country to another by locating the most casual national border in the world, on one side of St Peter's Square.

Off Pitch Tricks

TK-ed Off ☐ +6 for performing two of the following three tricks during a keepy-uppy session.

> You may not be the next Ronaldo, Rooney or Drogba on the pitch but you can impress off it with an array of outrageous football tricks. These are best performed as a keepy-uppy routine where you use any part of your body save your hands and arms to keep the ball in the air.

Footstall
The footstall is probably the easiest trick. As the ball rolls on to your instep (where your boot laces are), curl your toes upwards and trap the ball between your shin and foot. From this point the ball can be flicked back up for headers or knee bounces or can be used to perform a tasty around the world move (below).

Around-the-World
The around the world sees you pull your foot away and flick it up and around the ball fast to get back underneath the ball to catch it.

Shoulder Juggle
The shoulder juggle looks great and is deceptively simple although it takes practice. Flick the ball up and as you catch it on your shoulder, shrug your shoulder so that the ball flicks up to your head. Glance the ball on to your other shoulder which when

shrugged should send the ball back. Ten of these shoulder shrugs in a row look really cool.

 For more moves and advice, visit the fab freestyling football website Beyond Football at www.beyondfootball.com. And check out Mr Woo, the daddy of soccer skills at www.woosoccer.com and goggle with disbelief at his skipping rope, hotstepper and loads of other truly amazing moves.

2. Wild!

Heavy Petting

Get a pet and look after it well. You'll be better for it.

TK-ed Off ☐ +23

> Pets take day-in, day-out effort, but they can be enormous fun and quickly become part of the family. If you live on the ninth floor, don't ignore this challenge. A wormery, fish tank or hamster in a cage doesn't need a garden, a Great Dane or Shire horse does, so get some advice on what pet's best for you. The BBC has some excellent pet care factsheets at: http://www.bbc.co.uk/cbbc/wild/pets/

If you're not convinced that a pet is worth it, let me tell you about Reg. After Fluffgate (a guinea pig called Fluff bought for me when I was eleven, which died only days later on Christmas Eve), I didn't have a pet for over 20 years. Then Reg purrrrrrred his way into my life. This tiny tabby cat, scared of birds, deaf and almost blind was plucked from a rescue centre and has been my furry shadow ever since. I don't know what I'd do without him. That's what pets can be like.

Eat Something You Have Grown

TK-ed Off ☐ **+14** 'I ate a snack or meal mostly made from my own produce.'

TK-ed Off ☐ **+8** 'I grew and ate a fruit or vegetable.'

> **Nothing, repeat nothing, tastes better than eating a well-cooked meal with ingredients you have grown from seed yourself*.**

The choice of what you grow depends on the sun and soil conditions where you live. Even if you only have a window box or a few pots to play with, you can still grow a few items from fast-growing salad veg like radishes, lettuces and dwarf tomatoes to strong-flavoured herbs like chives and rosemary.

Contact your local council about allotment schemes which involve young people or ask around family and neighbours who may have some spare space. You might end up with a plot of land to grow crazy with!

---

*OK, so a really juicy cheeseburger probably tastes better, but it remains a great feeling to feed yourself with your own homegrown grub.

Flipper!

TK-ed Off ☐ **+28** 'I'm learning to scuba dive!'

TK-ed Off ☐ **+17** 'I've learned to snorkel.'

> Dive with dolphins? Yeah, yeah, yeah. I know it's the number one ambition on almost every list published. Not here at TK, though. We think it's so last year, it's not true. We also think it serves little porpoise (groan). It's all over in half an hour whereas our challenge – learning to Scuba dive – will last you a lifetime.

Scuba diving with an air tank, mask and flippers is a passport into an amazing and beautiful underwater world enabling you to travel down to see astounding sights – from old ship and plane wrecks to astonishing marine life. In the UK, the British Sub-Aqua Club (BSAC) is the main organization and they now have a minimum age limit of only twelve.

Their website (www.bsac.com) is a terrific place to start and lists all its local branches so you can find one near to you. Many clubs have Try Dive sessions where, for relatively little cost, you can get a diving experience in a swimming pool to see if it's for you. If you like it, you may be able to take lessons and trips with a club. The undersea world awaits you ...

Blag Box

Full-on scuba diving a bit too much? Snorkelling with a mask and flippers can be almost as much fun. The kit can cost less than £40, you can train in a pool with a more experienced snorkeller and then hit the sea shallows and view an amazing array of marine life. Dive into the pages at http://www.bsacsnorkelling.co.uk/ which contains some simple advice and a directory of local snorkelling clubs and courses in all areas of the UK.

Plant A Tree ... Then Another

TK~ed Off ☐ +8 'I planted at least two trees.'

> **Trees are simply amazing. They're the lungs of our planet, absorbing vast quantities of carbon dioxide, knitting soil together, trapping rainwater and providing habitats for a wide variety of wildlife.**

Humans must have quite some vendetta against trees because they – sorry – we, are hacking them down at a frightening rate; approximately sixteen football pitches of tropical rainforest, for example, every single minute. Madness. You can't reverse this terrifying trend by yourself but you can chip in and plant your own trees and, over the years, watch them grow.

Small trees can cost under a fiver and many nurseries offer even cheaper deals for buying in bulk so club together with others if you can. If you haven't got a garden, ask around, and see if you can plant trees at school or in your local community. Check out whether your local council offers any free tree schemes. Get advice about which species to plant and precisely where from nurseries and garden centres.

http://www.naturenet.net/trees/
Naturenet has links to everything about trees you'll need.

http://www.treecouncil.org.uk
Head for the Useful Information section on this site for an in-depth guide to tree planting provided by the Tree Council.

Swallow Your Pride and Say Sorry

TK~ed Off ☐ **+13** 'Yup, I did it and meant it.'

> We've all done it. Stuffed up, acted like an animal or made someone feel small or ANGRY. It might have been a harsh word, a broken promise or an act of vandalism such as doodling a marker pen moustache on your brother's prized painting or your sister's signed celeb photo. For my part, I remember really upsetting Julie Evans during biology when I laid out the eyes and guts of a dissected fish to make a smiley face on her desk. I laughed. She threw up. Not quite the response I expected. I never fessed up and said sorry*.
> Try to be quicker than me, eh?

1) Have a think beforehand. Put yourself in their shoes. Why were they so upset? What must it feel like? Understanding the other person and their feelings – psychology boffins call it empathy – will help.

2) No room for cowards. Don't email or SMS your apology. For it to work, you should do it face to face. Get the person alone, make eye contact, say you're sorry and mean it, really mean it.

*Until now ... Er, Julie, I'm, um, really sorry.

45

3) Allow time and space for their response. They may feel the need to explain why they were upset. They may just turn and stomp away. Don't expect an apology to make everything right instantly. But most times, if you back up what you said by being reasonable to someone afterwards, it can make a difference.

sorry

sorry

sorry

sorry

sorry

sorry

sorry

sorry

sorry

sorry

sorry

Jurassic Lark

TK-ed Off ☐ **+9** Scour shorelines to find something even older than your dad.

> And when I say old, I really do mean it. Britain's shorelines and occasionally forests yield up thousands of small plant and animal fossils that date to the Jurassic period (142-206 million years ago) as well as finds from the Cretaceous (65-142 million years) and the Triassic (206-290 million years back) periods.

The north-east of England and the south-east coasts tend to be the richest treasure troves of trilobites, ammonites and the like, but here are twelve of the best sites UK-wide.

⋇ Aberlady, Lothian – one of the best sites in Scotland and only 25 minutes from Edinburgh.

⋇ Whitehaven, Cumbria – good for plant fossils along its long shoreline.

⋇ Whitby – regular fossil-hunting walks and activities available.

⋇ Port Mulgrave, Yorkshire – if you don't find a fossil here, you're not looking!

⋇ Charmouth, Dorset – simply, this is fossil-hunting heaven.

⋇ Lyme Regis, Dorset – similar quality to Charmouth and with a cool visitor centre.

⋇ Folkestone, Kent – top fossil-hunting territory in clay soils.

⋇ Abbey Wood, London – need permission or go with organized tour to this site in South East London. (See: www.trg.org)

⋇ Hunstanton, Norfolk – a fossil-rich slab of coastline with towering, eroded cliffs.

* Llantwit Major, South Wales – Jurassic age cliffs hold many fossil finds.
* Mortimer Forest, Shropshire – a forest trail where you may nab a trilobite or piece of fossil coral.
* Colin Glen Forest Park, County Antrim, Northern Ireland – also check out the Ulster Museum for some big fossil finds.

 For other sites, ask at your local museums or head to these great sites for all things fossilized at:
http://www.discoveringfossils.co.uk/locations.htm and
http://www.ukfossils.co.uk
http://www.culture24.org.uk/science+%26+nature/dinosaurs+and+fossils

And the lawyers insist I must tell you ...
Shorelines and quarries can be dangerous places. Always go with an adult, make sure you have permission and follow all safety instructions at the site.

Fossil Facts

New discoveries in fossils are occurring all the time. Here are some facts fossil scientists are pondering over:

Fossil discoveries indicate that Sauroposeidon may be the biggest ever land dinosaur, standing up to 18 metres tall and weighing as much as 60 tonnes.

The oldest shark fossil was found in Canada and is a staggering 409 million years old.

Fossils of a giant 'terror bird' have been discovered in South America. The bird was about 3 metres high had a head as big as a horse and a beak 46cm long.

Go The Flamingo

TK~ed Off ☐ **+3** for performing the flamingo on your own.

TK~ed Off ☐ **+5** for performing it with one or more others.

> **Amuse those around the pool with a genuine synchronized swimming move. No sport gets the mickey taken more, so hold your nerve and impress those spectators with an Olympic-standard move, called the Flamingo.**

Float on your back, lift one leg out of the water and point it straight up. This move is called a 'ballet leg single'. Pull your other leg up to the chest to go the flamingo. From there, you can uncurl both legs so you're floating on the surface or drive your head under, stick both legs up vertically and dive gracefully downwards.

 Take a peek at the BBC Sport's excellent guide:

http://news.bbc.co.uk/sport1/hi/other_sports/swimming/7550273.stm

Why not invent your own outrageous moves and give them equally outlandish names? Add a bit of acrobatics in the finish, such as one swimmer standing on the knees of another and somersaulting off.

Animal Magic: Rabbit Not Required

TK-ed Off ☐ **+13** 'Finally, I've managed a magic trick.'

> **Did your last attempt to be David Blaine end in pain and no gain? Relax, here's one/two surefire trick(s) with an animal theme that are absolute no-brainers.**

Jumbo Danish
1. Pick a number between 1 and 10
2. Multiply it by 9
3. If it's a 2-digit number, add them together
4. Subtract 5
5. Now, count through the alphabet from the start until you reach your number.
6. Think of a country which begins with that letter.
7. Take the second letter of the country and think of a large animal which begins with that letter.
8. Think of the colour of that animal ...

Now's the time for you to ham it up. Appear to be thinking really hard, sway a bit and then say ...

'You're thinking of a grey elephant from Denmark!'

Chances are, they will be! You see, after that bit of mental maths, the number always comes to four which means that unless your friend opts for Djibouti, Dominica or the Dominican Republic, they're going to pick Denmark. And when you think of an animal whose name starts with the letter E, you're going to be pretty unlucky if your friend says elk. It's bound to be elephant!

Donkey Drag
Make an ass of friends with this painfully simply matchstick trick. Use five matches, cocktail sticks or similar. Make a donkey shape as shown and then challenge your friend to move just one match to make the donkey no longer face to its right but to its left.

Move the one match and the donkey's orientation has changed but he is now pointing left not right. APPLAUSE!

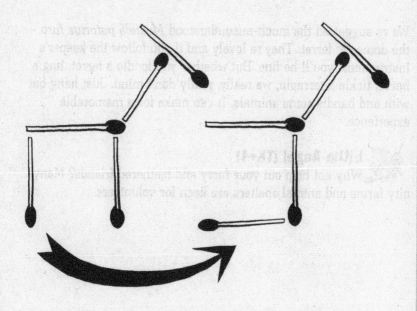

Fondle a Ferret

💰 ●○○○○ 😖 ●●●○○ 😩 ●●○○○ 👍 ●●●○○

TK-ed Off □ +11

> Seeing animals in a traditional zoo can be fun but
> there's always the wire netting or enclosure
> between you and the muskrats, wombats or
> meerkats. Visiting a hands-on safari park,
> city farm or nature reserve allows you to get up
> close and personal to a whole ark's worth of
> astounding animals.

We've suggested the much-misunderstood *Mustela putorius furo* –
the domestic ferret. They're lovely and if you follow the keeper's
instructions, you'll be fine. But whether you fondle a ferret, hug a
horse, tickle a terrapin, we really, really don't mind. Just hang out
with and handle some animals. It can make for a memorable
experience.

🐲 Little Angel (TK+4)
Why not help out your furry and feathered friends? Many
city farms and animal shelters are keen for volunteers.

Save A Million Centilitres of Water

TK-ed Off ☐ **+39** Brilliant!

TK-ed Off ☐ **+8** if you managed to save over 3,000 litres.

Water is essential to life. Saving a million centilitres (10,000 litres) of the stuff sounds virtually impossible but, trust me, it isn't.

A typical person in the UK uses 160 litres of water EVERY SINGLE DAY. Shocking stuff especially compared to people in the developing world who use fewer than 20 litres. The amount we waste is astonishing but so are the simple ways we can save vast quantities of water. Best of all, most cost nothing.

One of the best examples is cleaning your teeth. With the tap running, a two minute brush uses around 12 litres. Turning the tap off whilst brushing can use as little as one or two. Fine, Clive, that's up to 11 litres saved, just 9,989 litres to go. Yes, but imagine getting into that habit for a whole year ...

11 litres x brushing twice a day x 365 days = 8,030 litres. BOSH!

Interested? Well, get a notebook (recycled paper, of course) and jot down all the techniques you adopt and the approximate saving and keep a weekly tally.

✳ A garden hose or sprinkler typically uses 450 litres an hour.

Getting a water butt and using a watering can is harder work but can save all of that water.

✳ Skips to the loo account for about a third of all water used in a UK household per day. Each flush uses 6 litres, 12 if you have an old toilet. A water saver – a bag or plastic item which reduces the amount of water in the cistern tank – may only save one or two litres per flush but when you add up all the flushes, it's HUGE.

✳ Got a cold? Bin your bogey-ridden tissues, don't flush them, for more savings.

✳ A typical bath uses 90 litres, a five minute regular (not power) shower uses around 40 litres. Three showers a week saves 150 litres. Convince others in your house to follow and you're talking big savings.

✳ A tap not fully turned off or needing a new tap washer can waste as much as 140 litres a week.

✳ A washing machine uses around 120 litres per load. Make sure it is full or set to half load to reduce the number of loads used.

Watery Resources
http://www.environment-agency.gov.uk/

Lots of factsheets and advice under the water resources section of this wetsite (groan), I mean website.

Contact your local water utility company for their own water-saving tips.

How I Easily Saved A Million (and nabbed 49 TK Points)

Replaced one bath a week with a shower 50 litres x 52	2,600 litres
Fitted 1 litre water saver into newish loo Estimated 8 flushes x 365 days	2,920 litres
Used full loads for washing machine saving one wash every two weeks 26 x 120 litres	3,120 litres
Fixed one leaking tap 6 weeks before I would have done 6 x 140 litres	840 litres
Remembered sometimes (about 4 times a week) to stop tap running when brushing my teeth	2,288 litres
Total:	11,768 EASY!

Cheetah!

TK~ed Off ☐ +5 You bad boy or girl!

> Just once in your life cheat at something (not your
> school exams, though), take the credit and milk the
> glory. It might be a card game with friends or a general
> knowledge quiz where you just happen to leave your
> phone on under the table firing texts to mates asking
> them what is the address of The Queen Vic pub in
> Eastenders or what is the capital of Mongolia.*

It might be attaching a pipe to a growing marrow or squash running
into a bowl of sugar solution at the other end to fatten up a prize
vegetable in advance. It may simply be not fessing up to a great new
invincibility or extra power cheat on your latest PSP game that none
of your mates know about. We'll leave that up to you.

Enjoy the moment but see how you feel afterwards. There's every
chance it won't feel as good as a regular victory. You've done it now,
you've generated the story and memory for later. Now back to being
an honest citizen.

* 46 Albert Square, Walford and Ulaanbaator (or Ulan Bator), by the way.

Are You Sirius?

TK-ed Off ☐ +11

> Walking back in the great outdoors at night or
> waiting for a bus with someone you fancy? Tense,
> awkward silence? Run out of one liners? Don't fret.
> Things are looking up. Any boy or girl who can
> gaze at the night sky and point out some star
> groups (called constellations) suddenly becomes
> twice as interesting, romantic and spiritual.

First, the technical stuff.

Stars get messy with moving night skies but if you're north of the
Equator, you can always spot Polaris – the pole star. Face directly
north and look around halfway up the sky. The bright central star is
Polaris. The group of stars known as the plough rotate around it like
the hands on a clockface, so depending on the season, look in the
right direction:

✹ Jan–Mar – 3-4 o'clock   ✹ Apr–Jun – 12 o'clock
✹ Jul–Sept – 9 o'clock   ✹ Oct–Dec – 6 o'clock

Sirius is best searched for between January and June if you live in
the northern half of the planet. Face south and look low and to your
right. Sirius is the brightest star in that area and has a slight blue
tinge. Gaze higher and find three stars in a row which line up with
Sirius. They are known as Orion's Belt. Practise beforehand using a
chart of the night sky. For marvellous night sky charts go to:
http://www.fourmilab.ch/yoursky/

Second, the star quality.

It's all very well pointing out a few stars and sneaking an arm around the shoulder as you do so, but you need some star quality in your chat-up lines to really capitalize.

Do say: *'Sirius is the nearest star to Earth. It's also called the Dog Star.'*

Don't say: *'Sirius has a magnitude of -1.5 and is 8.7 light years from Earth. It's part of a binary pair and has the spectral type A.'*

Do say: *'I was talking to some Chinese people on holiday and they call the plough the Jade Balance of Fate. I wonder what our fate will be?'*

Don't say: *'Did you know stars twinkle due to large forces of air turbulence which, and this is fascinating, interrupt the flow of light from the nuclear fusion process happening in the star's central core ...'*

Don't moon around. Make sure you star at night and keep a small crib card in your pocket with the names of famous stars and galaxies.

Surf's Up

TK~ed Off □ +18

You don't have to reach Hawaii or Australia to surf wild waters. Many British beaches have safe waves ideal for junior surfers. Surfing hotspots include Bournemouth in the south, Tynemouth in the north-east, Llangennith Beach in Wales and Fistral, Croyde and Perranporth in the south-west.

Enrol in a surf school or plunge in with a spot of body (Boogie) boarding. Bodyboards are shorter and lighter than regular surfboards and are designed to ride waves on your stomach. Much easier to control than a surfboard, they're still great fun and timing your surge forward to get as long a run on a wave as possible can still remain a challenge.

Top Body Boarding Tips

1. Use a board with a safety leash to stop it speeding away from you and potentially hitting others.
2. Make sure your feet are underwater when you kick. Wearing flippers gives you more speed and power.
3. Lie on the board so that your hips just touch its tail. If you want to paddle with your arms as well as kick, hitch yourself up the board more and arch your back with your head up.
4. When you spot the wave to ride, paddle and kick hard in advance so that you're moving fast enough to catch it.
5. If you veer right to ride the face of a wave, hold the right-hand top corner of the board and put your left hand on the left edge of the board around halfway up.

Surf The Web

www.sup-surfing.org.uk/british-surfing-association/ – The British Surfing Association website with lots of details of surf clubs and beginners' guides.

http://www.waveblasters.com/videos.html – An awesome site full of excellent free instructional videos for bodyboarders.

3. So Simple it Hurts

Snog!

TK~ed Off ☐ +18

> You know you wanna kiss him or her. You're pretty sure he or she feels the same. Go on then, what are you waiting for?

Somewhere private and quiet is best so you can both concentrate. You don't need an audience for your first kiss. You do need to stay calm and focused.

No tongues. A first kiss should be gentle, sweet and relatively short. Try to avoid the clash of glasses or foreheads or using your lips like a suction pump.

Odour? Oh dear. Should have brushed your teeth thoroughly or used breath-freshening gum beforehand. Do remember to remove the gum before you kiss.

Groping is best avoided (well, at least at this stage). Just enjoy the moment.

Flan-tastic

TK-ed Off ☐ +9 Splatttt! Mmmmm

> **Make and deploy the perfect custard pie.**

Your pie can be as simple as a paper plate topped with lashings of shaving foam (OK) or whipped squirty cream (better). Or it can be as elaborate as a genuine custard pie topped with extra whipped cream and fitted with a second pie crust (Buster Keaton swore by the double-cruster so that the pie never crumbled as it was thrown). Always use a crust or paper plate as a base, NEVER a hard tin and remember, the flanning action is a gentle, smooth movement – it should never remotely hurt.

Angles of Attack and Rotation

Keep the pie parallel to the ground for as long as possible to stop gravity doing its thang and dragging your pie contents to the floor. At the last moment, angle your wrist so the pie edge closest to the floor is the first part to connect, touching your victim's chin. Follow through so that the interface between the pie and your target's mush is made squarely. Rotate your wrist back and forth 20-30 degrees or so to gently rub, not grind, the pie in. Flan-tastic!

U Devil: Two Times Pie (TK+5)

2 x Pie = the ultimate flanning experience in my opinion. As you line up your first pie face-wards, move round with the second pie and go for a low blow in the crotch. As your second pie swings towards its target bring the first pie up parallel with the ground at around neck height. As the victim looks downwards in horror you should be able to catch them full in the face. Delicious!

Enjoy your one-on-one flan flinging action, but check out the world's biggest custard pie fight which occurred at the Millennium Dome in 2000. A stunning, splattering 3,312 custard flans were flung in just three minutes. Outstanding!

Mope Opera

TK~ed Off ☐ +8

Secretly record someone having a tantrum and play it back to them a lot later when they've calmed down.

That's pretty much it.

It won't change the world, it may not shock the person who did all the screaming and shouting but you never know. What it will do is give you a bit of a thrill as you hope not to be caught filming at the time (either hide yourself or the camera). And after they've terrorized your household with their tantrum, the least the rest of you deserve is a bit of a laugh at their expense.

U Devil (TK+7)
You could, of course, burn the spectacular display of temper and childishness on to a DVD for repeat play. Alternatively, you could convert one or two of the most staggeringly unflattering stills of them in mid-rant into digital images and get them put on a mug or t-shirt as a present!

Little Angel? (TK+5)
Director, direct yourself. Choose a moment when you're seriously upset, retreat into your room, get the camera rolling and whine and moan on about how unfair your life is. Remember to review the footage at a later date.

Reality Cheque

TK~ed Off ☐ +26 You donated. Good on you.

You've just spent four hours cleaning horrible, sticky floors, delivering newspapers in the pouring rain or surrounded by the stench of stale burgers. That money of yours has been hard-earned and is earmarked for a fab new DVD or series of mp3 downloads. Forget it. Think of others and hand it straight to charity. Come on – you can afford it and look at the value for money you can achieve. Here are just four examples of the huge improvement in other peoples' lives your measly few pounds can make.

✳ £6 to Oxfam can buy 100 hungry children a dinner at school. It may be the only nutritious meal they get each day.

✳ £15 can be enough to give a blind person the power of vision via an operation to remove cataracts.

✳ £20 will feed three orphan children in many disaster-affected areas for a whole month.

✳ £24 can provide a goat to a family or village creating milk, meat, hides and breeding to create more goats!

Websites

Here are just three of the hundreds of charities you can donate to: www.oxfamunwrapped.com   www.actionaid.org www.comicrelief.com

Tat Attack

TK~ed Off ☐ **+11** plus 2 points for every two people you convince
it's a real one.

Let's face it. Real tattoos are a bit of a commitment
and may bomb horribly out of fashion in the future.
Imagine David Beckham on his 65th birthday –
those permanent tattoos of his are going to look
seriously sad on a grand-dad. A good quality
temporary transfer tattoo can look just as
convincing but with the massive advantage that it
lasts weeks and can be removed easily.

Temp Tat Tips
1. Read the instructions, apply carefully and have a spare in case
you stuff up.
2. Go for a small temporary tattoo in a discrete place such as your
shoulder. That's more likely to convince others it's a real one.
3. Splashes of water won't bother it, but try to keep it from getting
soaked to prolong its life.
4. Enjoy people's reactions to your new body decoration and see how
long you can keep the ruse going.

http://www.tattoofashion.com
Loads of designs at this website including a celeb's section
with tats – from Angelina Jolie's dragon design to Beck's Hindi tat
– all costing two or three pounds.

NB: NEVER have a Black Henna tattoo – people have been scarred
for life!

Make a Fuss

TK-ed Off ☐ +12

> We're all braced for gifts and nice things to happen
> to us on our birthdays. As kids and teens, you get a
> good deal, often being made a fuss of at loads of
> other times as well. Trust me, as you get older it
> happens less and less, which is a great shame.

So, do as you would like to be done by, and treat a neighbour, friend
or someone in your family when it's not a special occasion. Surprise
the old lady across the road with some nice flowers. Mate of yours a
bit down? Treat them to a night out or a CD you know they'll love.

Making a fuss of someone doesn't have to be a wallet-buster. Just
doing the cleaning up round the house unasked or laying on
breakfast in bed or a surprise dessert for dinner can raise the spirits
and a smile.

I'm Forever Blowing Bubbles

> Go on, blow the biggest bubble in history.

Top bubblers reckon it's all in the preparation. You have to work the gum in your gob really, really hard to soften it and stretch it as much as possible. Then flatten it hard against the roof of your mouth and your front teeth to get a large thin layer. With the gum resting against the back of your front teeth, push gently with your tongue through the gum so that a thin layer covers it.

Now go and blow. Remove your tongue and start to blow from your lungs not your lips. Remember the three Ss – blow slowly, smoothly and, er, continuously (make that two Ss and one C, sorry about that) to blow a big, BIG bubble.

TK~ed Off □ +4

'I blew a bubble about the size of a plum.'

TK~ed Off □ +7

'I blew a bubble as big as an orange.'

TK~ed Off □ +11

'I blew a bubble as big as a melon.'

Stage Struck

> Want to meet a star of the stage? Here's how to do it in three acts and with the following simple props: a show programme or leaflet, a working pen, a bag of top drawer sweets, a digital camera.

TK-ed Off ☐ **+9** for each star you meet and greet.

Act 1

Go to the show. Which one? The show your target star is appearing in, dummy. If you've already been, dig out the programme or head into the foyer or ticket office to grab yourself a promo leaflet.

Act 2

Find the stage door to the theatre. It's usually around the back and is where your star will depart after wowing the audience. Allow 20-50 minutes wait after the show's end. The door may be guarded by a minder.

Intermission

Remember those sweets you're carrying? Good. Smile sweetly at the minder and offer them a nice humbug, sherbert or piece of fudge. The minder may help you out or at least tolerate you standing around until the door opens.

Act 3

Be prepared to spring into action as your star appears. Now is your moment. Muscle in, smile, be polite and flatter the hell out of them as you ask them for an autograph and a picture.

U Devil (TK+5)

Get a piece of old-fashioned carbon paper. Place it on top of a piece of blank white paper and slip them both in the programme, a page below the one you want autographed. This way, you get two autographs for the price of one!

Share Your Secrets

You're a genius! You've discovered the chemical formula for chocolate that increases your IQ, located the lost continent of Atlantis or worked out why companies put an electric light in a fridge but not in a freezer. More likely, you've found a previously unknown hack or cheat in an XBox game, discovered an amazing music track no one else seems to know about, or a shortcut on your DVD remote which isn't in the instruction manual.

Whatever it is, good on you. Now tell the world.

Unlike crusty old Victorians whose idea of technology was steam-driven underpants, the 21st century offers you lots of ways to publicise your discovery – from post-it notes added to instruction manuals for your family to your own website, blog or YouTube entry where you can communicate with people all over the world.

TK-ed Off

☐ **+9** for sharing your secrets with others.

☐ **+211,907,455** if you really have discovered a lost continent.

Learn Your Faults

TK-ed Off ☐ +10 I'm amazed, apparently eating my own toenails appals
people.

You're great. You're amazing. But just like everyone
else, not only do you have faults and room for
improvement, you may not know what they are. In
between happy, fun challenges, and when you're
feeling confident, why not take on this lesson in
self-awareness and find out your flaws. Produce a
customer-service style questionnaire about yourself
and your habits, make copies and distribute
amongst friends and family. Be tough and honest
with your questions and leave them plenty of space
to answer.

When you're feeling brave, you will need the following: your room,
a hefty pillow or cushion and some loud music. Sit down in your
room and read through the answers. Now, you'll need the pillow. Give
it as many punches as you need to get rid of your anger at the
answers. Any screams or shouts you feel necessary will hopefully
be drowned out by the thumping tunes on your stereo. Once you've
calmed down, pay attention to answers which match up and say the
same thing. That's what you're going to have to concentrate on in
the future to improve!

Splat!

TK-ed Off □ +8 That sell-by-date-challenged trifle looked better on his head than in the bin.

This challenge is short but sweet . . .

... or spicy or sour depending what sauce is splashed and what food is flung. The perfect pie projectile (challenge no.33) might be a little too surgical and scientific for your tastes. This is meant to be chaos. In the right circumstances, outdoors after a summer picnic is nearly finished or when out of date grub is about to be thrown away, risk a carpeting and start a brief but explosive food fight.

It's not big, it's not clever, you will be told off, but if you choose the right situation, the grief you'll get will be far outweighed by the buzz.

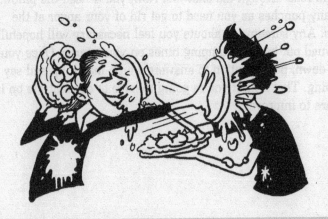

O.A.P. SOS

○○○○○ ○○○○○ ●●●○○ ●●●○○

TK-ed Off ☐ +9 'I helped out and I listened.'

> **Help an old age pensioner out. Why? Because it's the right thing to do and that will be you some day.**

How you help is up to you, or more accurately, up to them. Don't assume that just because they're old, stooped and wrinkled they're not independent or cannot speak for themselves. It may be as simple as helping them carry something heavy back from a shop (saving them an exorbitant delivery charge), a few household or garden chores, deploying your internet savvy to get them information they could do with or just simply, someone to sit and talk with.

Little Angel (TK+4)

Don't just do a good deed once, sit back and think, 'what a nice person I am'. Do good deeds often and regularly. They may take you a little time but they can make a huge difference to a person on their own.

The Language of Love

TK-ed Off ☐ +7

Some say there's no romance without finance. But if your wallet's crying out for assistance and you cannot afford a big treat, you can still impress him or her by going global with your compliments in as many different languages as possible. Here's a few to get you started:

Manyanga – a cute, attractive girl in Swahili
Me gustan tus ojos – 'I love your eyes' in Spanish
Du er deilig – 'You're gorgeous' in Norwegian
Kei te aroha au i a koe – 'I love you' in Maori
T'es trop belle – 'You're too beautiful' in French
Ja čjabe kakhaju – 'I love you' in Belarussian
Du wechst den Tiger in mir – German for, 'You arouse the tiger in me'. Er, steady on.

And finally, here's a bumper crop of translations for the magical sentence, 'Would you like to dance with me?'
Wil je met me dansen? (Dutch)
Maukah Anda menari dengan saya? (Indonesian)
Kas te soovite tantsida? (Estonian)
Tucheze ngoma? Utapenda kudansi? (Swahili)
A doni të vallzoni? (Albanian)
Viltu dansa vio mig? (Icelandic)

U Devil (TK+3)

Pick some foreign language insults (challenge 83) and pretend they're loving words. Unless they've read this book, they won't know what you're saying.

Fix Something Broken, Break Something Fixed

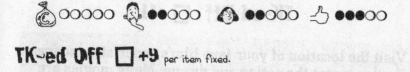

TK~ed Off

☐ **+9** per item fixed.

☐ **+6** for crockery carnage - we're feeling generous.

> **We live in a throwaway society. It's criminal really. So many things we own get chucked the moment they stop working.**

Sure, many of those objects are truly broken or are too expensive to get repaired but it's not always the case. Find things to fix from a fave pair of jeans which can be patched up to electrical items which just need a reset (read its instruction manual), a fuse, new batteries or a loose wire. Spruce up something shabby from furniture to a bike and search for or replace a missing part which makes something work again.

Now, the fun stuff. Once you've repaired one item, enjoy breaking something else. We're talking crockery carnage. Collect past-it plates and mugs minus their handles (but never glassware or mirrors). Ask at charity shops for any goods too damaged for them to sell. Set up a makeshift crockery shy like you sometimes get at fetes, and fire away.

Blag Box

Not got enough crockery ammunition for your demolition? Fake a major interest in Greece and badger your parents into taking you out for a slap-up Greek meal at a restaurant where you know (by ringing in advance) they perform traditional Greek plate breaking. Smashing!

Location, Location, Location

🪙 ●●○○○ 🧑 ○○○○○ 😀 ●●●○○ 👍 ●●○○○

TK-ed Off ☐ +11

Visit the location of your fave film's superlative scenes and re-enact the action and drama. Many movies are partially or totally shot in the UK. London, for example, has been home to a glut of movie scenes from *Batman Begins* to the amazing chase sequence along the Thames in the Bond film, *The World Is Not Enough*. Oxford was used extensively as a film location for the Harry Potter movies and the first Philip Pullman film, *The Golden Compass*.

You need to do some searching on the web and some scanning of your fave films to pin down precise locations. Two good starting points are dedicated official film websites and the Internet Movie Database (http://www.imdb.com). There are also many movie maps to be found for free on the web including an interactive UK-wide movie map at http://www.bbc.co.uk/arts/filmmap and a downloadable guide to some famous scenes shot in London at: http://filmlondon.org.uk/film_culture/film_tourism/movie_maps

There's also a massive collection of web links at http://www.movie-locations.com/

And for farther afield, try the excellent book, *The Worldwide Guide To Movie Locations* by Tony Reeves.

Diss Service

TK-ed Off ☐ +8

Received shoddy service at a shop, restaurant or mail order company? Don't start dissing them to your friends and do nothing else. Fight back and write back!

Contrary to popular belief, most customer services departments aren't staffed by morons or Martians but by decent people who will tend to respond to an articulate and fair letter (best done on a computer) from a disappointed young person. Be patient and wait a few weeks for a response.

Two Letters

Get it all out of your system with letter number one. Explain in long, droning detail all the anguish caused, how much you would like to lock them in a dark room with Crusher, the school bully and how rubbish you think their company is. When finished, read it proudly ... then tear it up and throw it away and write a brief letter to the point.

Outcome?

Why precisely are you writing and what outcome do you want? Do you want the item replaced? Do you want an apology? Do you simply want to let them know about a problem so that others don't suffer like you have done? Knowing the outcome you want will help influence the rest of the letter.

Fact Attack

Make sure you include all the vital data and facts like dates, order numbers and so forth in a short way. Don't be vague about problems. Try to be clear and specific about what is or went wrong.

Be Reasonable

As you write your letter remember that the person who will receive it and possibly act on it, isn't likely to be the one who caused you grief. A friendly, reasonable attitude is more likely to get results than a rant. End with the outcome you are after and that you hope to hear from them soon.

Here are two examples of the sorts of letters that make customer services staff put their head in their hands:

Dear National Lottery,

I bought a Win a Million scratchcard the other day. But didn't. You scumbags! How can you sell a crappy bit of card for a pound without the million quid coming with it. I couldn't help but smash up your display in the corner shop in anger. I want my million or there'll be trouble.

Yours Signed in Blood,
'basher' Evans.

Dear Sir/Madam,

I bought a tin of your Dehydrated H_2O the other day but the instructions say you just have to add water to make it work ....

4. Not for the Nervous

. . . .

44 45 46 47 **48** 49 50 51 52

Feel the Force

TK-ed Off ☐ +16

Ride the biggest rollercoaster in the world. Experience
stomach-churning anxiety on the way up and heart-
and-brain-pounding forces on the way down.
Screaming for your mummy is not an option.

The ultimate white knuckle ride at the current time is the Kingda Ka in New Jersey, USA. Boasting 950.4m of terrifying track action it is the tallest (139m) and fastest rollercoaster in existence and the first to shatter the 200km/h speed barrier. This beast unleashes 270 degree turns, giant dives and a rocket launch which propels you from zero to 206km/h in an earth shattering 3.5 seconds.

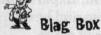 To stay up to date with what's the latest and greatest, head to the website of Intamin AG, the makers of Kingda Ka and other record-breaking rollercoasters. They can be found at:
http://www.intaminworldwide.com
And for more roller coaster information visit:
http://www.ultimaterollercoaster.com/

Blag Box
Can't afford a trip across the Atlantic? Head to Alton Towers which boasts two of Britain's best rides: Nemesis with forces of over 4G and the catapult launcher rollercoaster, Rita - Queen of Speed.

Have I told you Lately . . .

TK~ed Off ☐ +8

Rollercoaster or romance; fear comes in many forms. For some people, this challenge is more terrifying than being chased by a pack of rottweilers while wearing steak-flavoured underpants. There's someone that you fancy, right? Just nod if you're too timid to speak. Well, you're going to approach them and you're going to tell them that you like them, you think they're great and maybe, they'd like to go out with you some time ... There, simple, isn't it?

Try to add in a line about why you think they're great between your initial stuttering words and asking them out.

I think you're great because [circle where applicable]:
you make me laugh/you're really smart/you're rugged and handsome/you're kind and gentle/you're very pretty/your brother's got all the latest Playstation games and I want to come round.

A Ropey Challenge

TK-ed Off ☐ +14

Conquer your fear of heights to walk across a high rope bridge.

Despite rope bridges looking precarious, those found at adventure centres are exceptionally safe and often come with safety harnesses or crash mats underneath. Walk with knees flexed and soft footsteps along the bridge with your hands on the rails. Try to keep your head up and focused past the other end of the bridge. Looking down only unnerves and disorientates you.

To take it further (and higher), here are three notable bridges:

The rope bridge to Carrick-a-Rede Island off the coast of Northern Ireland is a serious nerve-shredder with the churning waters of the Atlantic Ocean below.

The Hochseilgarten (High Ropes Garden) in Kramsach, Austria is home to a staggering collection of different rope bridges, zip lines where you whiz down on a pulley, spider's webs and all sorts of ropey constructions. For more information, have a look at: http://www.forestpark.rittisberg.at

It's not strictly a rope bridge as it's made from steel cables but Capliano Suspension Bridge in British Columbia, Canada, is a must-do attraction. Suspended 70 metres above the Capliano River, the 137m long bridge offers amazing views ... if you're brave enough to take it on.

Halfway through the book now and with some tough challenges to come, you may be eyeing your TK ranking nervously. No one wants to be left floundering with a sub-100 score. So, here are a few self-explanatory challenges along with their TK points to help boost your score.

Visited Mars ... or any chocolate-making factory (TK+7)

Started a Mexican Wave during school assembly. Nice work (TK+11)

Half Time
TK Booster

Won a competition or got a letter or poem published (TK +8)

Recycled 100 glass bottles and saved enough energy to power your computer for 40 hours (TK+9)

Started a Mexican Wave at a sports event (TK+4)

Made 'amusing' animal shapes in the light from the projector in class or at the cinema (TK+5)

Appeared on TV as a contestant in a talent or quiz show (TK+14)

Stayed outdoors overnight (TK+3) cooking using an earth oven (TK+6)

Face Your Fear

TK-ed Off ☐ +2B 'I've faced and overcome a major fear of mine.'

We're all scared of something. In my case it's any puppy or pooch from the most dangerous Doberman to the tiniest terrier. I should say, 'was scared' because last year, I cracked it. Now, I feel a bit stupid (more stupid than I usually feel which is quite stupid indeed) that I'd been cautious of canines for so long. Overcoming a fear not only removes a barrier to every-day life, it also gives you a real boost in confidence which can spill over into other parts of your life.

Fact or fiction. Is your fear valid or irrational? Read up on your fear. For example, 99% of dogs never harm humans and the chances of coming to serious harm in a swimming pool with lifeguards and strong swimmers around you is incredibly tiny.

Assess your feelings about your fear. What genuinely are the chances of the worst happening? Why are you so scared? Think about this hard.

Confront your fear in stages. For example, if there is one particular dog you aren't scared of, get used to visiting it and petting it. If water on your face scares you, try splashing your face with water in the bathroom.

Environment. A controlled environment can help you face your fear. If heights are a problem, see if you can organize with a teacher a gym session where you jump and land safely on to crash mats. Special swimming classes for the scared exist in many towns whilst sympathetic keepers at a local city farm let you take your time in approaching and handling a creature you are nervous of.

The Little Book of Courage by Sarah Quigley and Dr Marilyn Shroyer and *What to Do When You're Scared and Worried: A Guide for Kids* by James J. Crist are two examples of the many books available to boost your confidence.

Under Pressure

TK-ed Off ☐ **+11** 'I went and did what I wanted to do and believed in, despite the jibes of others.'

TK-ed Off ☐ **+11** 'I refused to do something I didn't want to do, despite pressure from others.'

> Mates are great even if some of your mates' mates aren't. But sometimes what friends want to do and what they believe in will clash with you. When it's trivial such as choosing what to go and see at the cinema, be flexible, but when it's much more important, stand your ground and have the courage to do your own thing or not do theirs.

Don't, don't, don't shy away from doing something you secretly love or believe is right to do just because others reckon it makes you look a cissy, butch, uncool or sad.

Just as importantly, don't get roped into doing something if you really don't want to. It may be something dangerous, illegal, cruel or scary or it may simply be something you don't agree with. Stand up for yourself, refuse and walk away.

I Bet You Don't Look Good On The Dance Floor

TK-ed Off ☐ +13

> Clubs, discos and dance floors can be such achingly hip and serious places ... if you let them. Get out on the floor, show courage and dance exactly how you want. What's the worst that can happen?

You make a fool of yourself. Big deal. What if no one minds or even notices? We're urging you to go large with your moves and grooves, play the fool if you want, but most important of all, get out there and enjoy yourself. Who knows? The shapes you throw may be laughed at this week and then copied the next.

Go Retro

You could always bone up on break dancing so that you can pull some seriously old-school dance moves – from the up-rock to the swipe, windmill and hand glide. The place to go is http://www.i-am-bored.com/bored_link.cfm?link_id=8484 which has some simple but brilliant instructional animations.

Snow Business

TK~ed Off ☐ **+12** Weeeeeeeeee!

Slide down a snow-covered hill on a tray or bag.

You will need:
- A slope with a safe run-off area at the end
- Snow (durr!)
- A stout metal or plastic tray OR a strong bin bag
- Cycle or skateboarding helmet (and pads, if you're nervous)

Sure, you can buy fancy toboggans or snow trays but they're missing the point. A snowy slope is pretty rare in the UK and there's a real thrill in sliding down one on an ordinary household item. I've always favoured the bag over the tray, particularly a strong green garden waste bag. You can bunch up the top of the bag to give you something to hold on to. Choose a relatively gentle slope to get going and remember to let go and roll off your make-shift toboggan if you start losing control.

Warning: Ice may sound nice but you'll lose control. Make sure you only slide on snow.

Get Airborne

TK-ed Off ☐ +21

A flight on board a giant airliner can be great or grate depending on the food, film and how much the passenger next to you smells. If you hanker after a real feeling for the wonders of flight at closer hand, try to get airborne in something that holds only a handful of passengers.

A hot air balloon offers extraordinary views and smooth travel through the air although you may have an exciting, bumpy landing. Minimum ages can be as low as seven or eight but often balloon companies insist on a minimum height of around 4ft 6ins (137cm). Minimum ages for flying as a passenger in a glider and microlight tend to be older, around 14 or so. Often, the experienced instructor can give you some tuition and may let you hold the controls and instruct you on how to fly.

Blag Box
Sure, it's not the same, but the latest PC flight simulator programs are incredibly realistic and if a friend has the game and the control column with rubberpedals, you can get a real feel of flying before you really take to the air.

Battle of the Sexes: Render Gender Meaningless

TK~ed Off ☐ +25 'I stuck at what I like despite prejudice and nerves.'

Some activities are dominated by males or females. Buck the trend, hold your nerve and do what interests you even if you're the only boy or girl in the room, studio, garage or pitch.

You will need:

✳ A firm belief in your interest, ability and right to be there.
✳ A monk-like nature – don't rise to the sniggers and abuse.
✳ A knowledge of one or more top people in your sport or hobby area who are the same gender as you (a classic is to name check male chefs if you're a boy in a girl-dominated cookery club).
✳ A desire to prove yourself no matter what is said.
✳ Patience to keep at it and to make friends with the same interest.

Ladeeezzz

Get used to this cheesy heading
and similar comments from MCPs
(male chauvinist pigs) especially in
MCP-rife activities including
computing, cars and certain sports.
It's ridiculous, with lots of
successful women in these fields,
but if you'd prefer a torque wrench

to a make-up bench for your birthday, you're going to have to put up with these tiresome attitudes. Sigh, count to ten and carry on doing your best despite these bores.

Blokes

Get used to prejudice if you enjoy making clothes, sculpting a delightful soufflé, entering dance competitions or learning how to figure skate. In all fairness to the fairer sex, their attempts to snipe are likely to be dwarfed by the grief you might get from your own gender. Walk away, you're bigger and better than that.

Remember, the guys who shout the loudest are often the ones most envious of you having the nerve to do what you really want to do.

Jokes can help stop sexist comments. Here's two for each gender:

Why are jokes about blonde girls so short?
So boys can remember them.

What's the difference between a boy and a chimpanzee?
One is hairy, smelly, can't speak and scratches himself. The other's a chimpanzee.

What do you call a girl with just one brain cell?
Gifted

If boys and girls fell off a building, who would hit the ground first?
The boys. The girls would have to stop first to ask for directions!

Knock, Knock

TK~ed Off ☐ +5 'I knocked, I ran.'

Knock-down Ginger is the all-time classic prank. You're only young once, you've got to give it one go. The caring, sharing 21st century version only asks you not to pick on an elderly or infirm person. Instead, for maximum kicks, go for a worthy target, the front door of your PE teacher or the grumpy and scary mum of a loathed classmate.

Rap 'n' Run

Need instructions? You must have been abducted by aliens at birth, but here they are anyway.
a) Creep up to the door. The longer the pathway, the greater the challenge.
b) Give the knocker a good, firm triple rap or the doorbell a scarily-long four second blast.
c) Run!
d) Er, that's about it! Best done with mates as witnesses.

U Devil (TK +2)

Want to set up a mate? Know the phone number of the house you're going to knock on. Phone them up a few minutes earlier and prime the occupants. Send your mate in first to do the job and laugh at their surprise as the door is opened suddenly!

Play Identity Roulette

TK-ed Off ☐ **+9** *The youngest ever astronaut, you say ...*

> Liven up a deathly dull party by pretending to be
> someone or something you're not. See how long you
> can get away with it. It's some rush having to lie not
> once but a hundred times as you build your new life in
> real time in front of strangers.

To tell you the truth, I'm lousy at it. I start sweating, stuttering and get sprung in minutes. On the other hand, my friend, Chris, is a legend and has left a party having convinced all that he is a trainee astronaut, a naturalist working with gorillas in Rwanda and a failed internet millionaire who's lost his money and now lives in his car!

As an under-16, your choice may be more limited but you could pick to be a former child TV star, a world record holder (such as the youngest person to score a hole in one in golf), or the son or daughter of someone famous. Whatever you go for, pick something hard to disprove at the party and figure out good, strong answers to likely questions. Try to look people in the eye as you answer. You and your friends can back each other up, subtly with little hints or you can play a ruthless game of going it alone.

Poet and You Know it

TK-ed Off ☐ **+6** for completing a passable poem.

TK-ed Off ☐ **+11** for actually handing it to the person.

Write a love poem. Bin it. And then write a better one.

Forget flowers. Nothing declares your interest more fully than a love poem. Unfortunately, nothing tends to show up your English skills more, either. So, if your longest successful poem up until now was no longer than, 'Mel Smells' here are a few poetry pointers.

A Brief History of Rhyme
Your poem doesn't have to rhyme all the time. To be honest, it doesn't have to rhyme any of the time. Study different types of poems, from epic narratives like *The Rime of the Ancient Mariner* to the super-short three-line Japanese haiku to find a style that's right for you.

Plus Points Please
Concentrate on getting across some plus points of the person you're writing about. 'Your eyes are as dark as the sludge pit by the gasworks' isn't going to win you any affection, but reflecting on their glorious smile, their generous nature or the way they laugh will.

Compare Thee To Nature
Compare your love to various things found in nature, a staple of love poems old and new. Use objects and places from afar to make your writing seem exotic and from where you live which can make your

poem seem very personal. Be careful, though, here is how not to do it.

I wandered lonely, long and far
Until I reached the abattoir.
There an old dog gnawed at a bone
I thought of you and so wrote this poem.

Signed, Sealed, Delivered

Once you've completed your poem, sit on it for a couple of days and then read it through both silently and out loud. Chances are something will make you wince. Change it. Change everything you don't like. Once you're satisfied, write it out beautifully on some fancy paper, keep your nerve and send it.

U Devil (~5)

Stumped? Can't be ars**, sorry, bothered? Dock yourself 5 TK points and cheat, using one of the following three random poem generators. Remember to run the generator a few times until you get a poem that you like. Try, at least, to alter some lines and words to tailor it to your target.

http://links2love.com/poem_generator.htm
Type in your choice of fruit, birds, colours and noises, press a button and BOSH! Your own, albeit cheesy, love poem is generated.

http://www.dotsphinx.com/love.en/poems/
Similar to the above but with drop down menus offering you different options for each line.

http://www.everypoet.com
The excellent EveryPoet site has lots of poems and tips as well as an automatic haiku generator.

Grand Prix Free

TK~ed Off ☐ +23 for a four trolley or more grand prix.

> Abandoned supermarket trolleys in their thousands are
> a blight around Britain. Help your local area out and
> collect and return as many as you can find (pocketing
> the pound as a finder's fee) and have some fun with them
> beforehand. A survey by a well-known supermarket
> chain (I'm not allowed to say it was Tesco ... oops)
> revealed that British shoppers clock up 928 million
> trolley kilometres a year at an average speed of
> 0.8km/h. That speed's peanuts. Go far faster.

Organize a trolley grand prix in your school grounds or park (with
permission). Mark out a clear circuit on the grass and have teams
consisting of a driver and a passenger wearing safety gear. Decide
on the number of laps and allow teams to make pit stops a few
metres off the circuit to change drivers or refuel (i.e. have a drink).
You never know, done well, you may get a bit of interest and a
decent winner's prize from the local supermarket.

Pimp Your Ride
As the race organizer, you want to set the style on the starting grid
as well as, ideally, end the race as winner. Here's some pimping ideas:
Flames painted on card and fitted to the side of trolley with
gardening wire adds a dash of colour.

Old scoobies as tassles on ends of handle.

Spare bicycle rear view mirror can give you crucial views of racing rivals without you turning your head.

Airhorn or Horn can warn others or be tooted in triumph.

Choose your passenger carefully. They should be light but strong enough to push you if you run out of gas with just a lap to go.

Your passenger should stay low whilst racing moving side to side to help you take corners smoothly. Try out a few test laps to hone your racing style.

Little Angel: Load Of Rubbish (TK+11)
The average Brit throws away their own body weight in rubbish every three months. Fill the trolley with old rubbish and 'enjoy' a major calorie-busting workout pushing the thing to your supermarket's recycling area before handing in the trolley.

U Devil: Trolley Dolly (TK+2)
Been told off by your little sister or a female friend and feeling unfairly treated. Pretend to repent and offer them a ride to the local cinema. Keep schtum about the vehicle until the last minute then bundle her inside!

5. Live the Life

● ●

Bling 'n' Buy

TK~ed Off ☐ **+15** *I blinged my way in.*

> **Ever been snubbed for being a poor kid in a snooty big city shop or café and fancy revenge or, at least, gaining entry? Read on.**

Your Minder

For your minder, pick an older brother, cousin or pal who owes you a favour. Make them dress for success in a dark, sharp suit, polished black shoes, simple black sunglasses ideally with mirror lenses, and a tasty last touch, one broken in-earphone with the trailing wire cut leaving 5-10cm dangling. Long sweeping looks round with their finger just touching the earphone gives the impression of radio contact.

Fancy Dress

Now, you've got to look fabulous. Forget school disco or party. Think smart with a final flamboyant touch such as an outrageous fake feather boa, mega-jewellery or rakish hat (not a baseball cap or your gran's last knitted offering). A hat and high or stacked heels gives you extra height and authority.

Top Prop

Props-wise, you need one or two upmarket shopping bags, not pound shop numbers. Wrap up a few light items inside each bag in tissue paper to convince snooty staff that you've already been splashing the cash in other upmarket boutiques.

As an option, cut out lots of £10 or £20-sized pieces of paper. Make sure you have some real notes, nice, new and crisp, at the back and front of your wad and however small your in-store purchase, pay with a big note.

Store Entrance

You don't need to make a big scene on entering but you do need to keep your head up and exude confidence. Your minder should open the door for you and stand ahead, looking this way and that. When approached by staff, keep your answers short – a brisk, 'Just looking, thank you' should be enough. If you get your dress sense, attitude and your minder right, you should be able to browse as long as you like.

U Devil (TK+4)

If the upmarket eatery staff were particularly unpleasant to you last time, get them back by slipping a couple of dead insects into your overpriced salad, coffee or cola. Yelp and look disgusted as your minder does the complaining for you. At worst, you'll give them a start. At best, you'll get a free drink or meal!

Eat with Chopsticks for a week

Mealtimes duller than double maths? Easy. Try eating with chopsticks for a week. A third of the world's population use them for breakfast, lunch and dinner. Some scientists reckon that the smaller mouthfuls you take with chopsticks are good for your digestion too.

1. Crouching Chopstick

Put one chopstick between the palm and the base of the thumb, using your middle and fourth finger to help support it and keep it in place. The bottom stick stays still as you hold the top stick like a pen using the tips of your thumb and forefinger.

2. Leaping Lunchtime

Keep the chopstick ends even and spaced a little apart. Bring the ends together by moving the top chopstick with some pressure from your forefinger. The top chopstick pivots up and down so that the chopsticks work like a pair of pincers grabbing on to and holding a piece of food.

Practise on something chunky with some give in it like marshmallows before tackling teatimes. See how many meals you can manage. Obviously, if it's soup or rice pudding you're out of luck.

TK~ed Off ☐ **+17** 'Honestly, I did eat most meals at home with chopsticks.'

TK~ed Off ☐ **+8** 'I managed a few meals completely with chopsticks.'

TK~ed Off ☐ **~5** for stabbing your little brother/sister's arm instead of picking up your grub.

U Devil

Win a bet at school by picking up a peanut with chopsticks (regarded as a classic test of champion chopstick control). You can either do this by practising really hard or by spraying a peanut with a little glue that stays tacky and then switching the sticky peanut with a regular one when your friends have a try.

Docu-Gran

Document an elderly member of your family's memories in sound, words and pictures.

TK-ed Off ☐ +12

> Older people are amazing and have lived through some of the most momentous decades ever. Learn what they have learned and get to know more about them and their lives by researching and making a documentary on them. It doesn't have to be edited and polished. The key thing is to do all the research and interviews with them so that you can learn loads.

Give them plenty of time to think about it and to dig out their old letters, awards, photo albums and so forth. While you're waiting, sketch out what you would like to know and the questions to achieve this. You may want to know about distant relatives, their schooldays or what living through the 1960s was like. Try to make your questions easy to answer and have follow-up questions. That said, do allow them to go off-script as they tell you some fascinating facts from the past.

Allow plenty of time and conduct the interview over a number of different sessions. This gives you time to reflect on what they've said so far and think up more things to ask. It also allows them to get their breath back. Go through their photo albums with them and ask them about the people and events shown in the pictures. Photos can help jog a person's memory.

If using digital video, use the software to cut and paste the bits you want to use to make your documentary. Anything missing or not quite right can be re-shot.

Blag Box

Not got access to a videocam? Use a digital voice recorder or the record sound option on your PC or mp3 player to record their stories and memories. Burn them on to CD, add your notes and photocopies of any letters, photos or other documents that make interesting evidence. Bundled together, it makes a stirring document of that person's life.

Little Angel (TK+7)

As a thank you for their time, get one of their favourite photos enlarged and framed.

The Ex~files

TK~ed Off ☐ **+19** 'I was dignity personified. You would have been proud.'

TK~ed Off ☐ **+8** 'I lost it a bit at the time but recovered.'

You're going out with someone. You think it will never end. Check the stats on relationships. It probably will. Sorry. Didn't want to spoil you're day, but them's the facts. So what do you do when the break-up occurs?

> **Our challenge to you is to exit the relationship with your dignity intact.**

Don't blub, scream, shout or threaten your ex on receiving the news. If you feel like doing any of these things, walk away ... and fast!

If you're upset but in control, now's the time to ask for reasons if you're the enquiring type. Listen more than you speak. Unless, he or she is accusing you of something you really didn't do (like kiss his brother or stealing and wearing her clothes), try to keep any arguing back to a minimum.

Strain every sinew to part pleasantly on friendly terms. Any ranting, raving, crying and destroying of love letters or trinkets is best done, if at all, in private.

Remember for all the talk of heartbreak, your heart is a muscle and with exercise, it gets stronger. Run your upset off with some serious sport, a long walk or something else seriously distracting.

The first few days after a break-up are usually the hardest. Tell your best friends sooner rather than later and get them to help you through this tricky period. Expect tongues to wag, gossip to fly and people to prompt you to diss your ex and trash his or her reputation. Rise above it and don't give in to the temptation to spread rumours that her breath smells of toilets or that he wears underpants with the leg holes marked 'right' and 'left'.

Day four since the break-up. Kept your dignity? Well done. Now treat yourself with a present, a day out, whatever makes you happy. Move on, live your life and don't look back.

U Devil (TK+6)

Just because you've been cool, kind and dignified in public, doesn't mean you can't plot some gentle revenge. Keep it harmless and amusing and let only trusted friends in on the joke. Perhaps your gorgeous older cousin's coming from out of town soon. Bribe him or her to be your date, get your stories straight and flaunt your new partner for a night.

TV For Free?

TK~ed Off ☐ +13 for every month you meet your target.

> **Power your TV on energy saved through recycling.**

The power saved in recycling certain materials is staggering. Did you know that recycling one single empty aluminium can save enough energy to run your TV for three, count 'em, three hours. Stunning! It's based on the power-packed fact that recycling aluminium only uses 5% of the energy it takes to make new aluminium.

So, work out how many TV hours you notch up per week and divide by three to get your aluminium tin target. Start with your family's drinks cans but expand to take in littered ones on the street and at school. Get a café or shop that doesn't recycle to recycle, and then you're really cooking.

Mind you if your telly's on 24/7, you're going to need 2,920 cans to power it for a year, 2,928 if it's a leap year.

U Little Angel (TK +8)

See if you can convince others to recycle and set group targets. Try also to keep your TV out of energy-hogging standby or sleep mode. Switch it off completely when not in use. According to the Energy Saving Trust, the energy used by UK televisions in sleep mode is equivalent to pumping 480,000 tonnes of carbon dioxide (CO_2) into the atmosphere – that's more than created by three quarters of a million long-distance flights.

And why stop at cans: every nine glass jars or bottles you recycle add up to an energy saving equal to roughly three hours of telly time.

No Logo ... Own Logo

TK-ed Off ☐ +11

Most of us are brand junkies. Buck the trend, be a DIY designer and make your own brand clothing.

Keep things simple at first by using plain clothing. For uncomplicated designs a DIY card stencil and some good fabric paint will do the trick. Photocopy your design, stick it on to some stiff card and cut out the bits with a craft knife. Pin the stencil on the shirt and apply the fabric paint. Alternatively, you can design a logo using a computer and run it out on an inkjet printer using transfer paper. For those in the money, design online at websites like www.spreadshirt.co.uk

Coming up with your own logo or slogan can be the hard part. Puns and plays on words, like ASBO – Am Sensitive But Outrageous, or taking a well-known saying and subverting it, e.g. In Goth We Trust, can be striking and fun.

If you feel strongly about a subject, why not think up a slogan that reflects this. Keep any slogan short and punchy and not too rude, eh? Like your hair, but you're anti-war, how about, *Blondes Not Bombs* or *Skinheads Not Warheads*.

Small text across the middle of the shirt or over the left breast can look cool and convincing. A smaller version of your logo or slogan on the cuff of a short sleeve shirt can really enhance the effect.

Vegging Out

TK-ed Off ☐ **+11** for every month you go veggie.

> Many teen mags and books suggest limply that you should try going veggie for a day or week. Big hairy deal. If you're interested and have issues over meat production and consumption, go veggie for a month or three and by veggie, we don't mean cutting down the steaks to one a day with roast chicken on Sundays.

Before you make your decision, investigate the subject, learn what healthy and tasty alternatives are available to replace meat and inform anyone that cooks for you well in advance. This will give them time to faint, recover, worry about you and then listen to the results of your research. Once you've started vegging out, stick at it. Make some of your own meals to try out different things. You don't have to go mental for lentils, there are plenty of alternatives from mouth-watering curries, fritters and bakes to eager pizzas and veggie burgers.

If your reasoning for going veggie in the first place involves not harming living things, don't drift into scoffing tuna, cod and other fish or you'll stop being a veggie and become a pescavore!

Veg On The Net

The Vegetarian Society has loads of information including serious stuff on how veggie kids get all the nutrients they need. http://www.youngveggie.org/

Tips, advice and some really quick and easy recipes can be found at Viva's website (http://www.viva.org.uk/recipes/quick.html). Fancy walnut and avocado toast in seven minutes or Mexican tacos in a quarter of an hour?

Animal Aid has a massive collection of exciting veggie recipes including BBQ burgers, sweet potato wedges and veggie roast dinners. http://www.animalaid.org.uk/

U Devil (TK ~2)

OK, OK, you're desperately missing fish fingers, beef burgers or ham sandwiches. Try to resist, but if you're really desperate, munch your favourite meat for a meal and deduct two TK points from above.

Just the Ticket

TK~ed Off ☐ +11

Cannot get a ticket or not allowed to go to the big match or other major sports event? Forced to watch it on television? Well, liven up the experience and give it the big occasion atmosphere.

Get plenty of people over to watch the game, crammed round the wide-screen telly and wearing club colours, waving flags and scarves. Consider charging them a small amount and hand them their match ticket printed out on your PC printer. Have the TV volume up plenty loud to simulate stadium conditions.

On the referee's whistle, start the cheering and don't let up. Watch the game and see if you can get a mini Mexican wave rippling round the room if there's a dull moment during the game. If Chelsea are playing, there's bound to be.*

At half-time, recreate the true sports stadium experience with queues for the loo (if your house has two toilets, lock one!) and hot dogs or lukewarm pies all round for everyone.

Leave early or get several people to stand up so that others complain as the game continues.

---

*look, it's my book and I just don't like Chelsea, OK?

A Music Festival

If you've missed out on going to a massive music fest which is televised, try a similar approach to the above and recreate a mini-fest in your back garden. Run an extension cord to power a portable telly and some extra speakers for more oomph. Sit on the grass (the small telly approximates a live festival view), use plastic cups for drinks and see if you can have a barbecue going for that typical festival smell of wafting hot dogs 'n' onions.

Sign Time

TK~ed Off ☐ +15

British Sign Language is a remarkable language that has enriched the lives of tens of thousands of people who are deaf, hard of hearing or mute (cannot speak). It comes in two forms – finger-spelling where each letter of a word is spelt out using its own sign and signs which represent individual words, phrases or questions.

Here is the finger-spelling alphabet reprinted with kind permission from the RNID. Learn to spell your name and simple replies like 'yes', 'no', 'I don't know' and so on.

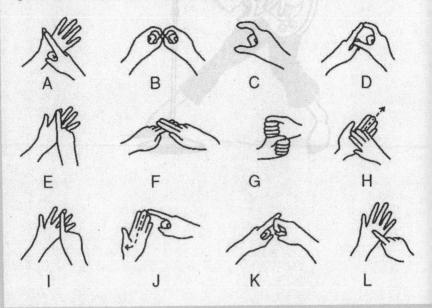

M   N   O   P

Q   R   S   T   U

V   W   X   Y   Z

For further information contact the RNID:
Telephone: 0808 808 0123 (freephone)
Textphone: 0808 808 9000 (freephone)
19-23 Featherstone Street,
London,
EC1Y 8SL
informationline@rnid.org.uk
www.rnid.org.uk

For further words and signs, check out
http://www.britishsignlanguage.com/ which features more than
400 common words.

Go Gourmet

TK-ed Off ☐ +15

> Gourmet food and fancy cooking are the new rock 'n' roll so why are you still sitting in the kitchen with the equivalent of a one stringed banjo – i.e. a disturbingly grey coloured microwaveable burger or a limp cheese sandwich with about as much zing as three hours of school assembly?

It's the 21st century. Jamie, Ainsley, Gordon and the rest of the boys have proven that gourmet cooking is not just for girls. And what better way to make your date think you're great than laying on a terrific three-course meal. We're not going to lecture you on what you should make. There are thousands of recipes out there. The key thing to remember is to not get too ambitious and cook within your limits. Go for something that sounds amazing and tasty but is in fact devilishly simple to make.

Preparation
Get some cookbooks out of the library and scan the pages for easy recipes that list short cooking times. Don't worry if preparation times are longer. Preparation is usually stuff like cutting, slicing, mixing and soaking – this takes very little skill, just a bit of effort.

Make your meal as foolproof as possible. Simple meals made with really good ingredients work wonders. Pick a dessert you can make in advance and a starter which is cold or a soup made beforehand so it's a no-brainer to heat and serve.

Presentation

You can make the greatest meal ever but if you slap it on the plate letting it all merge into a mess, you might as well not have bothered. Carefully place each part of the meal on a large plate. Some meals look great with a little portion of herbs or mixed salad leaves tucked on the plate or sauce drizzled (see below) around the edge.

What's In A Name?

There's a lot of nonsense about cookery and much of it is in the terms used. Bluff your meal up to sound more impressive than it is. A few handy words are below but if in doubt, work out the French for something straightforward – *oeuf brouillés* sounds so much better than scrambled eggs!

* **Blended** Two or more ingredients together. So as soon as you add water to something else, you have blended.
* **Drizzled** A fancy-dan term for poured really carefully and thinly (literally, to moisten with fine drops). An old jar with a small hole in its lid can make a handy sauce drizzler.
* **Roasted** Always conjures up impressions of quality but basically means chucked in a hot oven for a while.
* **Pan-Fried** Means nothing more than something fried in a pan – keep up!

So, 'pan-fried pork and herb-filled tubes served with butter-blended mashed *pommes de terre* with haricots drizzled in a rich tomato sauce' equals bangers, mash and baked beans!

Little Angel (TK+4)

Why not combine going gourmet with challenge no. 68? Check out veggie recipes in your gourmet cookbooks or head to the Viva website (www.viva.org.uk/recipes/winedine.html).

A~List for an Hour

TK~ed Off ☐ **+18** *I celebred my way in to the cinema. It was a riot!*

> Act like a serious celeb by making a grand entrance at a local restaurant, club or multiplex. Here's how.

1. Choose your venue: one that allows cars to stop for a few moments to drop people off right outside the door.

2. Get someone to gently mention to staff at the venue the rumour of a child or teen film or TV star visiting. Keep it vague enough that people can't go off and google the internet to confirm or deny.

3. Kit out several tall friends or suitable family members in classic celebrity minder gear (see challenge no. 62). Make sure you look absolutely fantastic. Serious shades are a must especially if it's gloomy or dark.

4. Arrive in style. A London taxi cab is acceptable but it's worth asking at a taxi or car hire company really close to your target venue if they have anything more sumptuous for just ten minutes. Alternatives are neighbours with a flash car or, if all else fails, a people carrier can look swish if a couple of adults wearing the full minder get-up, clamber out first.

5. If in an eye-catching car, try to cruise past the venue entrance a couple of times to drum up interest from the public. Make mobile phone contact with your team of stooges on the ground by the venue (the more adults and teens you can rope in, the merrier). Pull up

and wait for your minders to get out and open the door for you.

6. Take your time getting out. Your stooges are crucial now. Some, armed with cameras with flashguns, should be snapping away crazily. Wave generally, stop briefly to pose for a photo and move on.

7. Have at least a couple of stooges rush towards you as autograph hunters only for your minders to move them to the side. If the minders, photographers and 'fans' all move alongside you as you walk in, perhaps with you stopping to sign one or two autographs, they can give the impression of a sizeable crowd around you. Chances are at least one stranger seeing all the commotion will ask for your autograph, too!

8. How long you choose to keep the celeb style going is up to you. Personally, I'd change down in the venue and skulk away unnoticed at the end, but then, I'm a big coward.

Buy, Bye

TK-ed Off ☐ **+13** 'Loads of my old stuff has just sale-d away.'

> We live with soooooooo much clutter in our lives it isn't true. I'm something of a serial shopper so decided to stop the rot and started selling before buying.

Get Rid Then Bid

Before bidding on eBay and other auction sites, I vowed to get rid of something first.

Why not make a similar pledge using an auction site, free newspaper ad or car boot sale to sell stuff or donate things you don't want to charity shops? A number of stores run schemes in league with charities to reuse items like old spectacles and mobile phones.

Then there's the genius site, Freecycle (http://uk.freecycle.org/) which connects people who have stuff to give away with people who are happy to take it away.

Little Angel (TK+3)

If your local mobile phone or opticians aren't involved in a recycling scheme, politely ask them why not and watch them turn red. Ask again and get others to as well. With luck, if a few people ask, they might change their tune.

Big Buddha

TK~ed Off ☐ **+13** for seeing another faith's shrines or statues.

You may be religious. You may not. But you can still be inspired by the art and architecture of another faith and learn a bit more about that religion along the way. We've chosen the Buddhist religion and three giant statues of Buddha, as examples:

✳ **Leshan Buddha** – carved out of a cliff face in China's Sichuan Province, this is a monster at 71m high by 28m wide.

✳ **Tian Tan Buddha** – the largest outdoor seated Buddha in the world is found in Hong Kong.

✳ **Great Buddha of Kamakura** is a copper beauty over 17m high and found 5km or so south-west of Tokyo.

Blag Box: Other Icon Fun
If your wallet's idea of a trip to the Far East is Norwich, visit a famous religious icon closer to home. For example, the Shri Venkateswara Temple in Tividale, West Midlands, is the largest Hindu temple in Europe. Over on Merseyside, there's Liverpool Anglican Cathedral, one of the largest in Europe and home of a massive church organ with 9,765 pipes.

Oh, Oh Seven

TK-ed Off ☐ +3 for each technique used below.

Bond-proof your life with classic spy tricks and tips.

Being a teen sure isn't easy. Life is fast and complex, with rivals and enemies seemingly around every corner. What would a Jane or James Bond do in your situation? He or she would probably follow our [double] oh, seven tips.

1. Careless Talk Costs Spies
Be careful what you say. Bond always stays tight-lipped when he's not sure whether someone is a friend or foe. Others aren't so careful so build a network of informers (younger kids bribed with sweets are handy, but watch out for being double crossed) to catch up on careless talk.

2. Bugged!
Alliances at school and play can change so quickly, you've got to keep on top of things or you could be toast. Small binoculars can allow you to keep watch whilst a spy bug hidden in a normal-looking calculator (£15-£20) can transmit a conversation to a receiver some distance away. Secreted in the opposition changing rooms, it may reveal the other team's tactics. Hidden in your sibling's bedroom when their friends come round, it may give away who their fanciable mates like and dislike.

3. Code Safety
Need to send a message fast but fear it being intercepted? Make sure

it's in code. There are hundreds of ways of coding messages – the following website explains a few: http://www.youthonline.ca/spykids/ Alternatively, use some lemon juice and a toothpick to scrawl out your message which once dry will be in invisible ink. Gently warming the paper, i.e. putting it close to a light bulb for a while will reveal what is written.

4. Secret Lair

Think you've got nothing to hide? What about that secret interest in crochet you've kept from the lads or your personal diary or poems? When hiding stuff, be creative. Use Velcro or sticky pads to fit a sandwich box under a desk or chair and out of sight. Take an old, unwanted hardback book and cut out the central part of most of the pages. Glue the pages together to create a large hole in the book, just right for something secret.

5 & 6. Hair Raisin Intruders

Pluck a hair and stick it across the gap between door and frame. It should dry there and on your first visit back, its breakage or disappearance scream, 'Intruder!' A dried raisin in a plughole often expands if it's wet and will let you know if someone has run the taps for a while in your en-suite when they shouldn't.

7. Spy Another Day

Bond inevitably ends up beaten, bruised and tied up in his enemy's underground base seconds away from certain death, yet he always escapes. Remember, the films are fiction. If caught or cornered, forget your spy pride and RUN, leaving you safe to spy another day.

6. File Under ... Freaky

Pants on Parade

TK~ed OFF ☐ **+11** Pants Ahoy! Mission accomplished.

TK~ed OFF ☐ **+6** 'I set out my stall and made more than a fiver for the school. It was anything but all quiet on the Y-Fronts.'

> Got a school fete or sports day coming? Add to the decorations with some unexpected undercover underpant action!

You will need:
* Rope or strong cord
* A large pin board
* Photos of all your target teachers and other grown-ups
* Safety pins
* A prize (a book token, small box of chocs, that sort of thing)
* Pants

This last item is important. You need plenty of pairs of underwear and in as many different and horrid styles as possible. Check out charity shops for really big bloomers, tired old long johns and nasty patterned y-fronts. You're aiming for the most horrible, embarrassing pairs of pants in history!

String your motley collection of briefs and boxers
on the cord and secretly tie them up like a
piece of bunting at your fete. You've
got a choice now. You can either
chuckle, take a photo and run
away or turn those thongs and
tangas into a fundraiser.

This second course of action
requires a little bit of advance
work. Collect and pin up on your
board a collection of photos of
teachers and other adults you like
the idea of embarrassing mildly. Give
each photo a letter and pin a number to
each pair of pants and set yourself up as
a stall charging people to match all the pants allegedly to the parent
(or teacher or caretaker) on the photo board. The first person to get
all the matches right wins the prize.

Suffer from Wind

TK~ed Off ☐ +13 'I can play a tune on a nose flute or another strange instrument.'

Take up a strange instrument, practise in private so that you can later amaze and amuse in public.

There are dozens of truly weird musical instruments out there, from the vibrating Caribbean Marimbula to the Diatonic Bowed Psaltery (don't ask)*. Many are wind instruments such as the didgeridoo and the giant three-metre long alpine horn. Whilst we're all for freedom of choice here at TK, we reckon the Hawaiian nose flute (Ohe Hano Ihu in the native language) would be a good bet if you can find one. It's portable, relatively easy to learn with only a few note holes to keep open or closed and, OK, let's be honest, we reckon it'll gross a few of your friends out. The secret is to blow through your nose lightly (otherwise things could get a bit bogie-fied) over the flute's nose hole. Use your spare hand to both hold the flute close to your nostril and to press on the side of your nose to keep the other nostril shut.

Blag Box

A humanatone is a poor man's real nose flute made of plastic but costing no more than a pound or two. It still makes freaky sounds using both your nose and your mouth.

*Well, if you must know, head to: http://www.michaeljking.com/psalterymaking.htm

Super Grass

TK-ed Off ☐ +14

Fake a mysterious crop circle on your own lawn.

It's the summer hols and your mounting list of chores includes mowing the lawn. Add some E.T. intrigue. As your parents leave, make it clear you're off out yourself. That's your alien alibi.

As soon as they're gone, get the mower out and plan out your pattern which will be made from areas of grass you cut. Be careful to lift the mower into place so cutting or trampling en route to your site doesn't give the game away. For a basic circle, bash a peg in the ground at the circle's centre and tie a piece of rope to the peg and the mower. Guide it carefully round to complete the circle. By varying the length of the rope, you can make a pattern of concentric circles. Little flourishes like joining two circles with a line or cutting some straight or curving lines out from a circle are a nice touch.

Clean the mower, yourself and your clothes so there's no trace of evidence then abduct yourself round to your pal's house before your folks return. You've done no damage and can finish mowing the lawn at a later date. Make sure you get a photo of your extraterrestrial handiwork.

Take-Off Zebra

TK-ed Off ☐ +16

This is so, so not what you think, although if you manage to pilot a flying African plains animal, everyone here at TK would really, really like to hear from you. No, this challenge is quite different:

Put a bra on a cushion, pillow or outside a friend's clothes and time how long it takes you to take it off only using one hand.

Know Thine Enemy

Check out a standard back-fastening bra, the most common kind. It usually has two or three hooks or clasps on its back strap which lock into the same number of eyelets. See how they join and come apart.

Strap Attack

Start the stopwatch. Move your hand around the back of your pillow or pal. Feel for the thickening in the strap where the clasp is. Gently clench the strap either side of the fastening and leave a finger lightly pressing on the very middle. This will be your success detector. Squeeze the strap together gradually. Apply pressure until that finger feels the hooks and eyelets unclasp. Stop the watch. Well done! You are now a bra-barian!

U Devil

To up the challenge, try the same move under a layer of clothing – an old jumper put over the pillow, for example, or in the dark.

WARNING
Do not attempt this challenge on real bra wearers – it will most probably get you a slap around the face!

Salad Daze

●●○○○   ●●○○○   ●●●○○   ●●●○○

TK~ed Off ☐ **+13** 'Boy, I gave the salad bar a buffeting!'

Treat a one-visit self-service salad bar as a construction challenge.

Some salad bars proclaim they are ALL YOU CAN EAT but give you a lousy, small bowl and insist in a Scrooge-like way that you're only allowed one visit. What can you do, eh? I'll tell you what you can do. You can treat their miserliness as a challenge to your civil engineering skills. Cram in as much as you can. As a child, you may get a concerned look from staff, as an adult, you'd probably be told off, so now's the time to do it. And any fitness freaks out there, remember, we're talking about salad. A big bowlful isn't going to hurt.

Site Survey
Check out the ingredients available at the salad bar and however hungry you are don't rush in. Place your bowl on the bar leaving both hands free to work. Planning is crucial. I did the same and got some advice from a leading civil engineer who, for fear of recriminations asked to be given the codename, Mr Crouton.

Firm Foundations
Go for something sticky and heavy, like coleslaw or potato salad, at the bottom of your bowl and then select the stiffest long items on offer – breadsticks or crudités like celery or carrot sticks. These will be your exo-skeleton beams.

Room extension

'Cement' these beams in the sticky salad at the bottom so that they project a good distance above the rim of the bowl with a two to three centimetre gap between each stick. Fill in the gaps above the bowl with cucumber slices using a thin layer of sticky salad to bind them in place. You've just extended the room in your salad bowl. Congratulations!

Smarter Strata

With your bigger bowl, start adding the rest of the salad bar items you fancy, strata upon strata (a fancy way of saying layer upon layer). 'Take care to consolidate your layers,' advises Mr Crouton, 'pressing downwards with the back of your spoon to eliminate wasteful air pockets.'

Roofing

Keep the lighter items like cherry tomatoes and croutons near the top of your bowl. 'Too much load on the bowl extension could cause catastrophic failure of the exoskeleton,' warns TK's very own civil engineer who suggested the 'total weight of your construction can be boosted significantly by a timely application of 'void filler' also known as salad dressing'. Good advice as this adhesive covering can also hold bacon bits and croutons in place. Pop a few extra breadsticks in your top pocket and voila, your salad is complete.

Build a Buffet Bonanza

OctoPush

TK-ed Off ☐ +9 I watched or joined in an Octopush game.

> **Play a seriously 'out there' sport which is not only huge fun but unusual and attention-grabbing, too.**

Octopush is the name given to underwater hockey played along the bottom of a swimming pool with teams of six swimmers all wearing masks, snorkels and flippers. Players use their stick to pass between each other and drive the puck into the other team's goal. There are loads of teams around the country using local council swimming pools. The sport is actually played in 35 countries and the UK hosted the first ever World Championships in 2006.

Try out the official website for the British Octopush Association at: http://www.gbuwh.co.uk

Bonkers Britain

TK-ed Off ☐ +11

Maybe it's something in the water or the weather or just too much time on our hands, but compared to many countries we are bonkers, barmy, nuts, one gamepad short of a full XBox.

This is perhaps best shown in the vast number of downright ridiculous pastimes and festivities which break out all over Britain like a rash. Why not lay down your dignity and pick up the mad stick at one of these eccentric events?* Here's just a handful which tickled us. Use your local tourist information centre as well as websites like Strange Britain (http://www.strangebritain.co.uk/index.html) to learn about many more.

You Big Pudding
Early December sees the Great Christmas Pudding Race around Covent Garden with over 100 'athletes' running whilst balancing a Christmas pud on a flimsy paper plate and trying to avoid foam jets and flour-filled balloons.

On The Bog
Christmas pudding racing seems quite normal compared to Bog Snorkelling. Held in Llanwrtyd Wells in Powys, Wales every year, competitors have to travel through 120m of peat bog without using regular swimming strokes but still wearing snorkels and flippers.

*Although we wouldn't recommend taking part in the World Nettle Eating Championships at Marshwood in Dorset.

Toe Go and Conker

Every two years or so in the summer, the World Toe Wrestling Championship (you couldn't make this up) comes to Britain and is held at the Bentley Brook Inn in the Peak District. Autumn sees the nearby village of Ashton hosting the World Conker championships on the village green.

Bright and Brie-Zee

Perhaps the best known of all eccentric events, cheese rolling (racing giant cheeses down a steep hill) is rife in Gloucestershire at Coopers Hill, Brockworth. Events are held at different times during the year and there are under-12 boys' and girls' races as well! Check out www.cheese-rolling.co.uk for more details.

Pants On Fire

The World's Biggest Liar Competition is held in Wasdale in the English Lake District in Cumbria usually in November. Honest.

Neither are we lying about the World Pea Shooting Championships in Witcham near Cambridge, the annual weighing of the mayor of High Wycombe or the national dog freestyle dancing competition (See: http://www.caninefreestylegb.com/) held in Warwickshire in 2006 and Essex in 2007.

Okaasan Debeso!

> Or ... your mum's belly button sticks out – a mild insult in Japanese. Learn other mildly insulting or funny phrases (no swearwords, please) in some seriously obscure languages.

Help can come from foreign language guidebooks in the library and those who speak another language, the less well-known the better. Produce a handy card cheat sheet with some of your favourites on so that as someone spills your milk or calls you four-eyes, you have an immediate retort. Here's a few simple, silly and strange insults to get you going.

Albanian
Debil! – 'Idiot!'

Lithuanian
Rupuze – 'toad'

Indonesian
auah gelap kamu besar ayam – 'I don't care what you are saying, you big chicken.'

Croatian
Vrane su mu popile mozak – 'Crows have drunk his brain.'

Portuguese
Seu cheiro dos pés do queijo – 'Your feet smell of cheese.'

Japanese

Danga bana no kuma musume – 'You are a hairy girl with a dumpling nose.'

Be careful with your translations. Many famous big companies have stuffed up by not doing their research. For example massive car maker, General Motors advertised their new Nova car in South America but 'No va' in Spanish means, 'it doesn't go'! Beer-makers Coors' slogan, 'turn it loose' was translated into Spanish as 'suffer from diarrhoea'!

Thou rank onion-eyed minnow!

http://www.literarygenius.info/al-shakespearean-insults-generator.htm is a wonderful site that generates insults from the works and words of William Shakespeare and changes every time you refresh the screen. Check it out you 'yeasty boil-brained tottering tardy-gaited ratsbane!'

TK-ed Off +9 'Of course I insulted someone, you Debil (Korean for idiot')!'

Feeling Flushed

TK-ed Off ☐ +5

Perform a childish example of toilet humour before you're too old to get away with it. We've given a suitably juvenile, simple and freaky example below but feel free to think up your own.

You will need:
✳ A loo at a party or gathering
✳ A plastic worm or pale-coloured small, thin plastic snake
✳ A small inflatable cushion
✳ A piece of string

Tie the slim cushion under your clothes to look bloated. Make sure there are others in the loo queue behind you and groan and complain about feeling ill a little to set the scene. Once inside, make suitably gross noises, deflate and hide the cushion. As the flush ends, pop in the plastic worm or snake into the pan and close the lid. Leave the loo, look a bit embarrassed and rejoin the party but in view of the loo if possible to see the response. Sure you can work out the rest!

U Devil (TK+4)
Like your toilet humour? Take it to the trouser-trumpeting next level with a remote controlled fart machine available for under a tenner. We figure you can work out what to do with such a device!

I Wanna Hold Your Hand

TK~ed Off ☐ **+7** for every 'reading' you manage to get away with giving.

> **Learn just enough about chiromancy (also known as palmistry or reading palms) to bluff your way into holding his or her hand.**

Palmistry is an ancient art but genuinely no one knows if it's brilliant or bunkum. It centres on checking out the lines and other features of the palm of your hand and interpreting their length and shape although what these all mean can be a matter of debate. Exploit this by doing a little hand homework. Coupled with some cunning bluffing, you should be able to hold your target's hand for quite some time as you give a 'convincing' reading.

1. Head Line. The more the line curves downwards, the less control the person may have over their emotions. The bigger the gap between the head and heart line, the more confident and risk-taking a person may be.

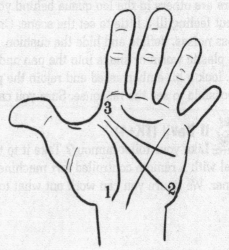

2. Heart Line. Loops, cuts and breaks in this line

show relationships, friendships and episodes occurring in a person's love life.

3. Life Line. There are lots of competing theories about this but in general, the longer and deeper the line, the more energy and vitality a person has.

Lots of fine lines on a hand show a complex, sensitive soul. The fewer the lines, the more straightforward a person is.

Surf the web or pick up a palmistry book to learn more.

Handy Hints

Explain how you need to examine both hands and spend your time poring over the palms carefully.

Think about the person beforehand and make sure that some of your comments are accurate but always veer on the side of flattering them. The more they like what they hear, the more likely they are to let you hold their hand for longer.

Keep it going for as long as you think you can get away with it but try to end on a dark secret or a feature you're puzzled by such as:

Hand Holder: 'Mmmm, very interesting ...'
Hand Holdee: *[Yawn]* 'What now?'
'Unusual, possibly, one of a kind.'
'What? *[More interested]* Really?'
'This line/cross/mound here, I think it shows your destiny ...'
'Tell me.'
'I'm not sure. It's very exciting. I'll have to check with my guru, can we do this again tomorrow?'
'Yeah, all right.'
RESULT!

Basho!

TK-ed Off □ +14

**Hold your own sumo wrestling competition.
U Know U Wanna Go Sumo!**

Sumo is an ancient form of ritual wrestling from Japan. In that country, the sport is huge, as are the competitors, often tipping the scales at over 150kg. Leading Sumo, Akebono Taro, weighed 235kg!

A *basho* is a sumo tournament and consists of a series of bouts. These take place in a 4.55m diameter ring called a *dohyō* and are often explosive, lasting just a few seconds. Competitors wrestle, push, grapple and try to throw their opponent. The first person to touch the ground with any part of their body other than their feet loses. The first person to touch the ground outside the *dohyō* is also the loser.

Use a loop of rope to make a *dohyō* outside, preferably on some soft grass. You'll need your good self, an opponent and at least one other person to act as *gyoji* (referee) and to help you prepare your sumo suits. In real Sumo, wrestlers wear only a thick belt (a *mawashi*) which runs around their waist and between their legs. This can be grasped by the opponent and used to lever the wearer out of the ring. Brings tears to the eyes, doesn't it?

Don't worry, we're not suggesting you wrestle naked or go on a gargantuan eating binge. What you need is some giant-sized clothing many, many sizes too big for you. An all-in-one zip up set of overalls for a giant would be ideal. Turn up the sleeves and leg holes and fill up every space possible by cramming in spare clothing, bundled up pants, socks, jumpers and cushions until you look like an inflated balloon. Alternatively, tie as many cushions and padded items all over your body with rope or cord.

Now, parade around the *dohyō* and throw a little salt into the ring to purify it, just like real sumo. Slap your legs as you plant your feet like the real deal, await the referee's signal and then perform a *tachi-ai* or charge.

Try to keep your legs flexed and your body position low. This helps keeps you balanced and makes it harder for your opponent to unbalance you or throw you. Look to surprise the opponent by, for example, dodging out of the way as they lunge at you and then push and heave them out of the circle.

Why not recruit as many friends as possible to your sumo competition to determine the neighbouring champion?

http://www.sumo.org.uk
It's a Japanese sport but yes, there's a British Sumo Federation.

Splendid Isolation

TK-ed Off □ +9

We planned for this challenge to be all about spending an hour in a flotation or isolation tank – one of those pricey and watery sound- and light-proof capsules you can lie in. Turns out that the swines who run these centres choose to deprive teens of the ultimate chill- out – the minimum age is eighteen and maximum height often 1.93m.

After cursing them we thought, why not create your own? Fill your bath with hot water, mixing in equal measures of bath salts and ordinary salt. Lights off, blindfold on, pop a set of earplugs in and, just for good measure, have some simple ambient new-agey music playing gently in the background. Lie still, relax and drift away without falling asleep. Let your mind wander and free itself of as many thoughts as possible. Many people find it really, really relaxing.

Blag Box
Free ambient music and soundscapes can be found on the internet, for example, at www.dreamstate.to/mp3s.htm or play with the relaxation tool at http://www.soundsleeping.com/

7. Maximum Kicks

Make or break an obscure World Record

TK~ed Off ☐ **+47** 'I'm an official world record holder!'

TK~ed Off ☐ **+23** 'I now hold a school, local or regional record.'

> You don't have to have been born brainy, freakishly tall or incredibly sporty to become a world record holder. You do, however, have to be single-minded, resourceful and possibly, downright sneaky.

Flick through a copy of a recent *Guinness Book of World Records* at a library and see if you can spot a record that looks ripe for tackling. Some records have attracted enormous interest making them tough to beat. Anyone got 4,002,137 dominoes on them to beat the current toppling record?

Other records may be more vulnerable, especially massed-participation events like the world's largest Twister game (27.1m x 8.43m). Get your school involved using magic words like 'publicity', 'teamwork' and 'community' and you'll have teachers eating out of your hands. Guinness are strict about what they accept (terms and conditions are on their website). There are many other records monitored by other organizations, such as the *Book of Alternative Records*, available from book stores.

> Niek Vermeulen holds the world record for the biggest collection of airline barf bags (empty, thankfully) - 5,034 of the darned things. Sick!

Seek out a record area such as 'biggest collections' or 'most people' and try to find something that isn't listed. It could be the biggest collection of bus tickets or tea bags or the most people all playing the same tune on a recorder. If you see a gap, go for it, and good luck!

Six Steps To Success

1. Research well to pick the best record to go for.
2. Read and follow the conditions of a record attempt.
3. Share your idea with others who can help. Sadly, adults will have to be involved.
4. Patience and persistence are the keywords, whatever record you go for.
5. Document your record attempt with witnesses, photos and so forth.
6. Be patient as your record is ratified (checked on). If you manage it, celebrate!

Record Breaker Websites
http://www.guinnessworldrecords.com/default.aspx

Blag Box: Break A School Sports Record
Check school sports records, there's bound to be a complete gap somewhere from no times for the under-14s 800m or 1000m to no record of most goals in a game or season. Have a go at establishing a first record making sure a teacher is around to witness the record. Even if it's broken later, you were the first record holder.

> The world record for the largest number of people dressed as gorillas in one place is 637!

Sunny Delight

TK-ed Off ☐ **+17** for each one of the destinations below
you manage to visit.

Wake up and see the sun rise or set somewhere beautiful
and very, very special. Here are our top eight dawn or dusk
destinations although there are many more.

The Taj Mahal
Sunrise or sunset makes for staggering views and pictures of this
beautiful building and its ornate gardens, located 200km south-east
of the Indian city of Delhi.

New York
The Statue of Liberty and the soaring skyscrapers of the Big Apple
look astounding in the half light especially from a point around New
York Harbour.

Machu Picchu
The majestic lost mountain top city of the Incas, Machu Picchu is
extraordinary at any time of day but sunrise gives brilliant colours
and lets you look around before the biggest crowds arrive.

Grand Canyon
The stats are amazing (466km long by up to 29km wide by more
than 1500m deep) yet still don't do it justice. A place of awesome
beauty, it's best seen at sunrise from an east-facing vantage position
such as Yavaupi Point.

Tokyo

Japan's capital city is a fascinating and often beautiful place. Check out the sunset from Ueno Park, the Imperial Palace or the gardens surrounding the Meiji Jingu shrine.

Lakes 'n' Lochs

The stretches of water in the Lake District and the Scottish Lochs reflect the early or evening sun beautifully. Sitting shoreside or cruising in a boat on Loch Fyne, Loch Lomond, Ullswater or Bassenthwaite Lake, to give four examples, is a truly memorable experience.

Serengeti

Sunrise or sunset at Tanzania's premier wildlife park is a must to see African wildlife – from wildebeest and hyenas to cheetahs and elephants in abundance.

The Canadian Rockies

On a bright clear day, the view from the Rocky mountains can only be described in one word, breathtaking: check out Lake Louise near Banff with its extraordinary emerald-green coloured waters topped up from nearby mountain glaciers.

And to make sure you don't miss either dawn or dusk, head to http://www.timeanddate.com/worldclock/sunrise.html which gives you times for dozens of locations around the globe.

Chute to Thrill

TK~ed Off □ **+27** 'I flew up, I jumped down. It was awesome.'

TK~ed Off □ **+8** 'I loved it so much, I did it again!'

> When it comes to parachuting, you have to be sixteen or over to jump from a plane in the UK, USA and some other countries – sorry! But now's the time to begin a campaign to make a parachute jump your sixteenth birthday present. How cool would that be? Your folks do have to be onside as you need a signed letter of consent if you're under eighteen.

Parachuting, or skydiving to give its sporting name, is a big deal in the UK and Europe with dozens of centres and with beginners' training and first jump costing £125-£240. Your first jump will come after some drilling from qualified instructors. Mostly, they'll work on you making the right shape as you leap out of the plane, learning to steer the parachute and your landing technique so that you don't injure your legs, particularly your ankles, on impact.

Up in the air, you'll be jumping from an altitude of around 1,000m using a static line parachute. This automatically opens after you exit the plane leaving you free to recall your instructor's words, to adopt the right body position and to check your chute canopy.

I jumped when I was eighteen and it was the biggest buzz imaginable – terrifying and exhilarating at the same time. Leaving the plane is only matched by the magical views as you descend and the rush of making a good, safe landing. The thrill will stay with you long afterwards. You've managed to do something many only talk about.

Jump Tip

Ask the instructor to use your digicam to get some photos and videos of you making the jump.

http://www.bpa.org.uk/
British Parachute Association – the organization that governs parachuting in the UK.

Tower of Power

TK~ed Off ☐ **+13** *'I'm on top of the world, Ma.'*

> ## Stand astride the top of one of the world's greatest toweringly tall monuments.

There are loads of famous tall buildings and structures around the world. Make it your mission to reach the top of at least one of the most famous and fascinating before you turn sixteen. Three great examples are given below but there are others including the giant Petronas towers in Malaysia, the Sears Tower and the Statue of Liberty in the United States and the AMP Tower in Sydney, Australia. In all cases, make sure you take your camera and binoculars to capture the sights from the top of the tower.

Get an Eiffel of This
The 322m Eiffel Tower is a world icon. Everyone knows its shape. Enjoy a Parisian workout by taking over 700 steps to the second floor before hopping on the lift to the top.

Empire State Building
The building stands over 380m tall and has 85 floors of offices. The 86th floor is the world-famous open-air observation deck which has magnificent views of New York. Check before you go, to see if the observation deck on the 102nd floor is open.

CN the Sights
Found in Toronto, Canada, this is the world's tallest tower with an observation deck, If you've gone all that way, make sure you get a ticket for the Skypod viewing point, a giddy 447m up. Also, check out

the slightly scary see-through glass observation deck at 342m up and the amazing revolving restaurant which completes a full 360 degree circle every 72 minutes.

Blag Box

Contact your council and local tourist centre to find the tallest building or structure in your area. Many, like the Blackpool Tower and the Spinnaker Tower in Portsmouth, have public observation points. Some others don't, but this is where you set your powers of persuasion to stun, write as creeping a letter as possible to those who run or own the building and see if you get lucky and get an invite to the top. Being a school kid is a distinct advantage here.

Hi-Rise Websites

http://www.skyscrapernews.com/ukstallest1.htm

The excellent Skyscraper News website which lists the tallest buildings in a large number of British cities.

http://www.openhouse.org.uk/openhouse/home.html

A brilliant scheme where every September, hundreds of buildings normally closed to the public in London are opened up.

Run for Office

TK~ed Off ☐ **+18** If you ran an election campaign regardless of whether you won or lost.

> **The position may range from school president to guardian of the class hamster, but if several others want to do it as well, push for an election and then trounce them with a slick campaign.**

You can learn a lot about how the real world operates when you take part in an election. Give it your best shot, try to develop a thick skin in case you don't get elected and do be gracious in defeat.

1. Build an election team around you. Get plenty of mates in who are willing to help and get them to start networking amongst the different cliques and groups at school. Even in school-wide elections, candidates often focus on their class or mates. Look wider than this for your support.

2. Younger or older brother, sister or friend at the same school? Brilliant. Give them a title they're proud of, Deputy Head of Strategy and Communications: be nice to them at home, and get them to start building support amongst their year.

3. Start your campaign early. Work out what you can offer that your opponents cannot and shout such things loud and clear (e.g. you want to look after the school pets and you live next door to a vet).

4. Work on a catchy slogan and key policies – the things that you are offering to the voters. Make these as enticing as you can but don't promise what you can't deliver unlike many adult politicians.

5. Get posters and fliers designed, printed and in circulation before your opponents. You will set the agenda meaning that your opponents may have to start responding to your ideas and policies rather than advancing their own.

6. If you're not good at speaking in public, try something different. Record your speech in the privacy of your own home and set it to a stirring soundtrack. Play it on speech day or offer it to the voters beforehand as an mp3 file.

7. Keep some of your poster and flier budget back. This will allow you to respond to your opponent's posters with a final push.

8. Get one of your team to report to teachers any dirty politics from other candidates such as defacing your posters, bullying or bribing voters. Don't resort to bullying or bribes yourself.

Ramp It Up, Pipe It In

TK-ed Off □ +26

Ride the freshest powder at the most extreme snow-boarding locations on Earth.

If you know your McTwist from your Caballero and use wax for your board not your legs or hair, chances are you're a committed snowboarder. Aim high and make your ambition to visit a major competition like the X Games to see the pros in action as well as carving the slopes and grabbing big airs at the world's best places for snowboarders, five of which are mentioned below:

✱ **Chamonix, France** – beautiful scenes, packed with experienced snowboarders and lots of space to cruise and freeride.

✱ **Whistler-Blackcomb, Canada** – huge variety with over 230 marked runs, twelve alpine bowls, three large halfpipes and two terrain parks.

✱ **Mammoth Mountain, USA** – arguably, the best of all, this Californian park hasn't stood still and has recently unveiled the world's biggest pipe. The monstrous Super-Duper Pipe has seven metre walls and is a ridiculous 200m long.

✱ **Les 7 Laux, Isère, France** – freestyle and obstacle heaven at this compact but exciting park with loads of rails, table tops, pipes and other great obstacles.

✱ **St Moritz, Switzerland** – Glitz and glamour is guaranteed at this swish Swiss resort which has great half and quarter pipes as well as freeriding runs.

> **Blag Box**
> Ski pants pocket empty of Euros or dollars? Visit one of the UK's booming range of indoor snowparks instead. These include ones at Tamworth (www.snowdome.co.uk), Milton Keynes, Glasgow and Castleford (http://www.xscape.co.uk) with the Chill Factor in Trafford Park, Manchester and several others in the [half] pipeline.

Skip to the Louvre

Get an Eiffel of the art at the Louvre but don't start moaning about Lisa.

Paris is a top city; top for romance, top for history but especially top for art. Many of its most stunning art objects are crammed under the roofs of the world-famous Musée du Louvre.

The Louvre's treasures include Leonardo da Vinci's legendary Mona Lisa. Up close and personal, it's surprisingly small, but other pieces of art around the place are whoppers. The Wedding at Cana by Paolo Veronese is a huge 9.9m wide by 6.6m high! These are just two of the thousands of objects housed in the Louvre's 8km of corridors and chambers. No one's expecting you to see them all, but do spend a few hours wandering around. Download a free guide (see below) and read up before your trip.

TK-ed Off

☐ **+11** 'I went to the Louvre and saw the Mona Lisa plus . . .

☐ **+6** The Wedding at Cana painting (and counted over 130 people in it.)

☐ **+2** The Venus de Milo sculpture

☐ **+2** The marble sculpture of the goddess Nike, known as the Winged Victory of Samothrace

☐ **+4** Works of art by Van Gogh, Da Vinci, Rembrandt and Raphael.'

Blag Box

Visit the Musee d'Orsay (add 8 TK points) whilst in Paris. It's the home of hundreds of famous paintings particularly by Impressionists such as Claude Monet, Edgar Degas, Pierre-Auguste Renoir and Paul Cézanne. It costs a fair few Euros for adults but for under-18s it's free!

Check out the museum website at:

http://www.musee-orsay.fr/en/home.html

http://www.louvre.fr

Select English language (top right) and enjoy the official website for the Louvre is packed full of details.

http://www.parisnotes.com/museums/parismuseums.html

A really handy website with downloadable guides to the Louvre and other museums.

Make a Difference

> Work towards changing something for the better – from your own inner calm to having a stab at helping your community or the entire world.

Relax! Be A Serial Chiller   TK~ed Off ☐ +12

You live a high-paced, high-stressed life. If it isn't dealing with peer group pressures and endless homework, there's a dull, dreary part-time job and your infuriating parents. You need to calm down and chill out. Why not try yoga or a meditation class? Yoga isn't about tying yourself in knots (well, not really). Hatha yoga, the type of yoga usually found in Europe, involves practising getting into different body positions (called *asanas*) and using different breathing (*pranayama*) and meditation (*dhyana*) techniques.

Taking up yoga works for girls *and* boys. Many sportsmen, from Monty Panesar to Roy Keane, and dozens of leading boxers and rugby union players swear by it. Over time it will improve your flexibility, muscle strength and peace of mind. Check out your local leisure centre for classes.

Volunteer!   TK~ed Off ☐ +21

You may have a high-paced, high-stressed life but it's sheer luxury compared to the lives of many. Help out those less fortunate than you by volunteering at a local homeless centre, hospital or charity group. www.do-it.org.uk/ is a great starting point listing volunteering opportunities both by the subject and by local area so whether you fancy helping stray dogs in Catford, working with the elderly in

Oldham or planting trees in Sevenoaks, the opportunities are out there.

Protest!   TK~ed Off ☐ +15

If there's something you believe strongly in such as animal welfare or the rights of people with disabilities or something you are strongly against such as gangs and guns or pollution, do something about it. There's a pressure group or charity for every conceivable issue and most are on the internet. Join a group or learn where to send a written complaint of protest.

Scrubber!   TK~ed Off ☐ +19

Graffiti, vandalism and dumped rubbish can ruin a canal, pond, park or any facility in your neighbourhood. Join forces with others to scrub, dispose of waste and generally clean up your community. Writing to your local council may also see them supply new equipment and materials to improve the area as well.

Is Statue? ... Yes!

TK~ed Off □ +38 *'My oh my, those Moai were amazing.'*

> **Visit the most mysterious, isolated island on the planet – Te pito o te henna (the island at the navel of the world), also known as Rapa Nui or Easter Island.**

Dotted in the middle of the Southern Pacific Ocean, Easter Island lies over 3,000km away from any other inhabited land. Somehow, primitive but ingenious peoples in tiny canoes found and colonized this speck of rock. What they left behind was truly awe-inspiring – over 800 partially-made or completed giant stone statues, called *Moai*. The largest would have stood 21m high and weighed over 300 tonnes.

Dotted round the coast or found in the stunning volcanic crater quarry, *Rano Raraku*, these distinctive statues are a beautiful part of a major mystery. How did peoples with next to no metals or technology build them and why? How did they move them round the island? And what of the islander's mysterious sign language, Rongorongo, which no one has yet been able to decipher? It all adds up to one of the most fascinating places on the planet.

Travelling from Chile or Tahiti to reach the island is not cheap – Easyjet and Ryanair don't fly there – but it may be something to plan for in the future. Those who have visited remember it for the rest of their lives.

Save Your N.R.G.

TK-ed Off ☐ +34 *'I saved a million watt hours in six or seven months. Genius!'*

Electricity usage is often measured in watts (w) per hour. How about saving a million watt hours in six or seven months? Impossible? You are so, so wrong. Follow the ideas below, keep a rough record of your success and see if you can make the target in as few months as possible. It really is as easy as ABC ... oh and D.

A) Light Right

One 100w light left on 24/7 uses a huge amount of energy – 438,000 watts in six months. Do a quick light audit around your house seeing how many lights are left on unnecessarily and approximately for how long. A strict switching off regime can easily save over 1,100 watts per day, **saving 200,000 watt hours** in six months.

Get your parents to replace lights left on overnight with eco-saver bulbs which may only use 12 watts instead of the 60w bulb you currently use. Fitting two of these bulbs can save 768 watt hours per night. Over six months, that's **140,160 watt hours**.

Replace an often-used 100w bulb with a 20w eco-saver. Assuming typical usage of eight hours a day, that's another **116,800 watt hours** saved.

B) Standby

Turn off/unplug your mobile phone charger when not in use. They tend to use around 5w per hour which if left permanently on and in place equals a whopping **21,000 watt hours** per six months. Get someone else in your family to follow suit and you're saving **42,000 watt hours**.

Check out other items with standby features like televisions, DVD players and set top boxes. Switching them off when not in use or recording can save thousands more watts as well.

C) Screensaver Off Energy Saving On

A computer screensaver is precisely that, it looks after the screen but only cuts the power used a little. Switching your monitor off overnight can save **175,020 watt hours** in six months. Add in switching off for periods during the day and when you're away at weekends and on holidays and that can double to **350,000 watt hours**.

Whilst you're at it, power down your PC and any peripherals like printers, modems and powered speakers when not in use. These can typically save you 400 watts a day or over six months, **73,000 watt hours**.

D) Other Savings

Switch off electric fan heaters when not needed. They consume 1000-2000 watts per hour. A typical 60 hours less use over six months saves another **120,000 watt hours**.

Don't blow a thousand watt hours by using a washing machine to wash one or two items. Full loads less often over a six month period can easily save you **40,000 watt hours**.

A kettle may only be on for a couple of minutes but is a fierce user of electricity. People regularly overfill a kettle for just one or two cups of water. Using the right amount of water can easily save **30,000** or **40,000 watt hours** in six months.

98

Be Part Of The Olympics

●●●○○ ○○○○○ ●●●○○ ●●●●○

TK-ed Off ☐ **+28** 'I'm getting involved!'

Forget Euro 08, the Commonwealth Games or even the FIFA World Cup. The world's biggest event, sporting or otherwise, will be hitting our shores before you know it.

With the cream of the planet's sportsmen and women, over 11,000 of them, going for gold in events varying from heavyweight weightlifting to extreme white-water kayaking, the 2012 Olympic Games will be like no event ever held in Britain. The Olympics have visited these shores twice before, in 1908 and 1948, but both games were low-key in comparison to what's in store come 2012. With more nations keen to host the games, this is likely to be the one chance in your lifetime to see and be a part of the games in Britain.

Save in advance and apply for plenty of tickets for the events you most want to see. Not all of the events are in London – check out sailing in Weymouth and men's and women's football in Manchester and Newcastle. Eight million tickets will go on sale but they will go faster than a gold medallist sprinter. Also treat yourself to tickets to lesser-known sports. See the International Olympic Committee (www.olympic.org) for more details.

Do more than just spectate at the games, get involved. Check out the many school and youth initiatives and other events which will be launched in advance of the Olympics. You may be old enough in 2012 to volunteer for the games. Some 70,000 volunteers will be

chosen in 2010 and trained to assist. Keep going back to the official website to check for breaking news and events. It's at: http://www.london2012.com/en/gettinginvolved/

I Want My Mummy!

TK~ed Off ☐ **+26** 'Wow, I saw the Nile in style, was a geezer at Giza and took a look at Tut's tomb.'

Go pharaoh with a holiday in Egypt. Package deals are relatively cheap, especially for out of season breaks and your folks can do their thing such as chill out in the sun whilst you visit some truly astonishing sites.

Cairo has the biggest museums and is the perfect launch pad for the awe-inspiring pyramids of Giza. There are also other pyramids to see at places like Saqqara and Dahshur. Many fans of ancient Egypt, though, head south to the city of Luxor the site of the majestic Karnak and Luxor temples and close to the astonishing Deir-el-Bahri temple and the awesome Valley of the Kings and Valley of the Queens, home to the tombs of many Egyptian pharaohs.

Why not start planning the places you'd most like to visit in Egypt by checking out the following:
http://www.touregypt.net/egyptantiquities/
A massive website with huge amounts of information on all aspects of Ancient Egypt with maps and photos of key sites.

Produce a modern art masterpiece

TK-ed Off ☐ +26

> Like we know how to. If we did, we'd be opening a gallery and making more money than JK Rowling. What you can do though is have a go at creating something bold, stirring and different from what you've seen before.

> Warning: Modern artists - please, please look away now. A big part of modern art (and if a gaggle of modern artists catch me, they're going to pickle me in formaldehyde for saying this) is the highly creative way their work is explained and put in context. The simplest piece of art can be turned into something profound in some people's eyes with an epic explanation best printed from computer on to white card.

I once went to the Tate Liverpool and watched a video of a conceptual artist putting on layer upon layer of clothing until he was almost perfectly round. I also saw retro-wrestler Kendo Nagasaki's mask, but that's another story. The point is that modern artists work in all sorts of materials, known as media, from collages of photos and performances of art to video, stone and recycled rubbish.

So, experiment with different materials and try out your own ideas. Visits to modern art galleries can inspire you but try to come up with your own ideas and reasons for producing your art.

Warning: Modern artists - please, please look away now.
One of the great things about modern art is that it has allowed many artists with no great talent at drawing or painting to get stuck in. This is grand news if your still life sketches make your art teacher cry (and not with delight) or even your highly sympathetic gran snort, 'Drawing, call that a drawing, why in my day...'.

A chunky cheese grater with a joke shop bloody finger glued to its blades sounds like a bit of old nonsense, but given a lofty title such as: 'When Metal Meets Membrane' and described as, 'signifying the clash of unfeeling and brutal modern industry with the most basic sense in nature, that of gentle touch,' starts to sound like the real deal. And with a 50p DIY store light fitting fixed to the grater and a light bulb inside making the grater act as a novel lampshade, you can suddenly throw in all sorts of other meanings.

If there are empty bits in your art such as the hole in a doughnut you've glued to something, use words like 'void' 'emptiness' and phrases like, 'signifies the hollow centre of everyday existence'. We could go on, but we won't as by now, surely you get the picture ...
... or sculpture or video or installation, don't you?

> 'Juxtaposition' is a good word to squeeze in to your art explanations. It means placing two or more objects side by side often to compare and contrast.

TK~ed OFF ☐ +14 for a fully-fledged art attempt.

TK~ed OFF ☐ +27 for making something which gets exhibited and taken seriously.

Star at Something

> You've got this far. You're a star. You deserve to shine.
> Pick one of these top notch TK challenges to
> finish off with.

And The Winner Is ...   TK~ed Off ☐ +24

The Oscars, Mobos and Brits are all very well but unless you're a
child star or live next door to the Kaiser Chiefs or Tom Cruise, you
can forget blagging a ticket. The solution, like your school bully, is
devastatingly simple – host your own awards ceremony. Think gold
and silver for envelopes and spray paint to turn ordinary, cheap items
into awards (silver spanner, golden eggcup) whatever suits the title
and theme of your ceremony. Pick your categories and nominees
carefully and assemble as big an audience (free food 'n' drink helps)
as you can. Come the glitzy big night, you can play the host or sit
safe in the knowledge that you'll win a major award – after all, it was
you who wrote the nominations and winners.

Make Your Own Movie   TK~ed Off ☐ +31

You need bags of time and energy as well as a real artistic vision to
do something different from the thousands of movies and videos out
there. You also need a high quality webcam or digi-vid, movie editing
software on PC or Mac and pals prepared to help in different ways
from providing locations or props to appearing in your film. But if
you can put it all together and be bold, thoughtful, daring and
different, you have a potentially massive online audience on places
like YouTube.

Take heart from a simple 75 second video in 2006 by teenager Melody, aka Bowiechick, which has been watched by well over 200,000 YouTube users and saw her interviewed on live TV. Take it further with a course or working with other young film-makers and who knows, a decade from now, you might be the new Spielberg, Lucas or Coppola.

Gagging For It   TK-ed Off □ +28

So you think you're funny, eh? The true test is to perform a stand up comedy set (five or ten minutes) in front of real live people with a pulse, not that collection of dolls, cuddly toys and action figures you laughably call an audience*. Study DVDs of top comics in action and rehearse your set of jokes rigorously so that you know them inside-out. Five or ten minutes may not sound much but on stage it can be an eternity. Start with a couple of short, punchy gags, amongst your very best, to get the audience going (well, hopefully).

Have a put-down or two prepared in case of hecklers (shouts, comments and jeers from the audience). A couple of mildly insulting ones are, 'Does your carer know you're out?' and 'We could have a battle of wits but it appears you're unarmed'. It's vital though that you utter your put-down and then move straight back into your set. Don't indulge a heckler or you'll get waylaid. Aim for a big finish with your funniest couple of jokes, thank the audience and exit fast. You've done it!

---

*Mind you, it's amazing how Barbie's beady eyes can stare right through you when during rehearsals you forget or fumble a punch line.

Well, you came, saw and maybe, conkered. Perhaps you snogged and blogged, dressed for success or found love, fossils or your inner calm. Good on you. Tot up your TK points and turn back to page 5 to get your ranking.

But it doesn't have to end there, does it? See if you can boost your TK tally over the next few months. A couple of major challenges tackled, a couple of minor ones bagged and you'll see your TK ranking soar.